Andy Martello's

Stupid Stories

About Famous People

By Andy Martello

Just A Martello Books
Las Vegas, NV

Andy Martello/Just A Martello Books
andy@andymartello.com

Book cover layout and design by Suzanne Fyhrie Parrott
SuzanneFyhrieParrott.com

Edited by Amanda Schrader, Mandieland Literary
mandielandliterary.com

Book Layout ©2013 BookDesignTemplates.com

1st edition.
ISBN 978-0-9970456-1-1
Library of Congress Control Number: 2016919771

To Matt Martello
Had he not suggested these ridiculous stories, told
mostly over drinks with friends, would make a good
read, I may not have bothered with this book.

To Melissa
If I didn't have someone to forget, I would never have
written about someone to remember.

To Don and Wyn Martello
For always supporting me in my entertainment career,
even though I certainly could have been a good son and
become a doctor or something respectable.

Chapters

CHAPTER ONE

Almost Famous

As luck would have it, I am not famous. Not one bit. Not even the tiniest of amounts. Sure, I've been on television and in a few movies. Yes, I have published a few award-winning books. I have been seen on my fair share of red carpets. I have been an Honorary Duck Master at the Peabody Hotel, and I have signed a hot dog bun at the world famous Tony Packo's Cafe in Toledo, Ohio. None of this means I am a celebrity of any kind. If there is an A-List in Hollywood, I would have to be somewhere on the ZZZ-List.

I have headlined a show in Las Vegas, and I do continue to work in shows on the Strip and on Fremont Street, but that *barely* makes me Vegas Famous; That phenomena by which every entertainer in Vegas is considered to be famous, even when they are clearly not known outside of the city. I have always believed, though, that I am the most famous non-famous person in the world. Google my name and I am like a rash all over the Internet. It's as if the latest computer virus is Andy Martello and nobody, even the snooty Mac users, can get rid of me or deny my existence. That being said, I am not at all famous.

I do *look* famous for some reason or another. Maybe it's because I've been a working entertainer for 30 years. Perhaps, it's because I groom well and carry myself like a seasoned performer. I can't really say why. I just know I often get asked if I'm *somebody*. I offer you one of my favorite conversations I had with a lovely lady at a bar one night:

HER: Are you famous?
ME: If you have to ask, then I am probably not famous.
HER: Well, you look famous.
ME: Then, yes. I am very, very famous.

I have a number of celebrity friends in my phone's contact list. However, that is only due to my association with the world's most (genuinely) famous game show. As the announcer for *The Price is Right LIVE!* I have only toured the U.S. and Canada entertaining untold thousands of people, and I've been fortunate enough to work with quite a few different celebrity hosts from Jerry Springer to Joey Fatone. I have a rather unusual and eclectic list of people I may now call friends.

I find there is one burning question people have asked me since I started out in showbiz: have I met, and do I have any cool stories about, celebrities. People love to hear about my encounters with those considerably more famous than I. These are the stories that make my friends laugh, the ones I am asked to repeat most often, the ones people seem to want to hear – even if I they aren't sizzling or tawdry. People simply want to hear about what it's like meeting or working with someone noteworthy.

For this reason, I chose to write this book. Believe me, this is not an attempt to prove how cool I am. There is no ego-stroking involved here, apart from my getting to say, "*Yay!* I wrote another book!" I have no grudges requiring me to exact revenge, and this isn't a tell-all book designed to make a quick buck. These are stories about my, oftentimes, brief encounters with various celebrities. Whether I was working with them, or I happened upon them randomly in the world, these are things that happened during those tiny moments. Most are worth repeating because they are funny or entertaining in some way, some because I learned something life-changing as a result of the encounter. For the most part, they are simple, fun stories designed to make you smile.

I believe most people end up with a few stories like these. Lord knows I have heard plenty of, "Hey! You'll never guess who I ran into at the grocery store!" recollections over the years. Thanks in part to my long-running career as an entertainer, I have more of these types of stories than most people. I have to say that I've been fortunate; not just to have met these people, but that I've walked away from these experiences with good stories. I truly believe stories are what matter most as the years go by, and I learned while writing my first book — *The King of Casinos* — stories are what make a book, a program, and a life more interesting.

I am grateful to have lived an interesting, and mostly positive life thus far. As the years go by, I smile when I turn on a TV program or a movie and find myself saying, "Hey! I know that guy," or, "I worked with him!" It also makes me happy when I get opportunities to relay these stories to people and they are met with enjoyment. What I shall recount in this book is only a small part of the moments in my life worth repeating. Do I have as many tales as someone who is actually famous? Of course not.

This might also explain why I don't have any juicy, sordid tales involving drugs, hookers, or orgies. Maybe in the next life.

Some of these musings will be familiar to long-time friends, the rare reader of my once-busy-but-now-nearly-extinct Tales from Andy Land Blog, or readers of my weekly columns at websites like TheCheers.org. I have tried to expound on the memories for you and embellish as little as possible, although I may be guilty of a little harmless creative license here and there. A good story still needs a good storyteller, after all. One thing I can promise is that these stories are all true to the best of my recollection. Even if you do not find them terribly exciting, I am rather hopeful you will find them entertaining. If not, what did you expect from a man who's not at all famous?

CHAPTER TWO

Original Sins

Unless you are related to someone who is famous, I am fairly confident in saying most people's first encounters with the well-known, the notorious, or the influential comes as a child. When you are very young, the first famous person you are likely to meet is Santa Claus, the Easter Bunny or any of the strolling costumed characters at a Disney, Six Flags, or some other amusement park. Of course, we all know these are not according to Hoyle celebrity sightings.

I think everyone tends toward the awestruck in some way when it comes to celebrity. I can't think of too many people who don't have at least one celebrity story they're willing to share if the subject comes up. It seems everyone has a famous person in their family history or, at the very least, believes they were a celebrity in a former life. If they don't have a personal story, most have a wish list of people they would love to meet. Many couples, while they may not admit it publicly, have a "celebrity exemption" clause in their relationship consisting of a list of acceptable celebrities their partner could sleep with if, by some miracle of happenstance, the opportunity arose. Don't scoff, I know you have one. If you don't, you *want* one. Admit it.

Popular opinion of the well-known — how they are perceived by the average person — seems to be determined by how a celebrity reacts to the excited fan. We've all heard tales of the movie star who's a lousy tipper and the wonderful rock star that was really nice when a giddy fan completely lost control in their presence.

I never believed my family was prone to any sort of celebrity-based awe. I found out I was wrong. Whether or not it really happened, I recall my father speaking with great reverence about the time he met poet, Robert Frost. I was a small child at the time, and had no idea who he was talking about, but my father took pride in relaying the memory; that sense of pride lead me to learn a little something about Mr. Frost. Apparently, he was a writer or something. I kid, I kid!

Both of my parents have spoken about some noteworthy relatives in our family. If I am to believe the stories, we are somehow related to William Shakespeare's wife, Anne Hathaway, as well as being distantly related to Charlemagne himself, Charles Martel. The only other times I remember my parents being impressed with celebrity had to do with meeting prominent sports figures, particularly if they played for Cleveland, Cincinnati, or Chicago teams.

Mythological or cartoon icons notwithstanding, if you were fortunate enough to have parents who took you to professional sporting events, your first real celebrity sightings probably came from hunting for autographs at a baseball stadium or another sporting arena. I am certain that's where I had my first notable encounters with noteworthy people.

Growing up in rural northern Illinois, I was a huge fan of the Chicago Cubs. Watching the games on WGN became something of a ritual among my family members. The players and announcers alike became big celebrities in my eyes. This is the reason I think fame has a lot less to do with visibility, and more to do with name recognition. Yes, being on television every day will play a major part in upping your celebrity status. However,

there was a time when I idolized people like Larry Biitt-
ner, Ivan DeJesus, and Barry Foote. None of these players are Hall of Famers, and I wouldn't be able to pick
them out of a police lineup unless they still look exactly
like their era-specific baseball cards. Yet, I remember
their names to this day. To me, they will always be famous. Certainly more famous than I am.

The Cubs were playing the Dodgers the very first
time my parents took me to historic, pastoral Wrigley
Field in Chicago. The Cubs won 4 to 3, and I remember
thinking that everything about the experience was more
spectacular than I could have imagined. The field itself
has always been an iconic figure. Were it possible for me
to get the building to sign my program, I surely would
have done so.

I was eager to search for signatures with my dad and
my little brother, and the quest began before we even
entered the stadium. We got to the ballpark early to wait
for the players to get off their bus before entering the
park. It adds a lot of time to your day, but the players'
entrance was a very cool place to see *everybody*. Of
course, if you didn't know what the players looked like
out of uniform, it made things a little difficult for the
novice autograph hunter. I recall asking several people
for signatures, only to find out they were cab drivers,

parking lot attendants, and other baseball fans. Eventually, we got the hang of things, and dad would laugh watching us chase after summertime heroes in the city.

One time, when the Giants were in town, we learned a little bit of autograph etiquette. We managed to track down the great Joe Morgan quite by accident. We had no idea who he was, but he was in a suit, so . . . We handed him an item to sign and a blue Bic pen. He took the item to be signed (a Cubs tote bag from a previous game), but refused to take the pen. He just stared at it as we held it impatiently in front of him. "You can take the cap off, son," he said. Embarrassed, I quickly tore off the cap, and he was kind enough to sign the bag. Lesson learned. Always remove the cap for the superstar.

We went back to tell Dad our embarrassing tale and show him the autograph. He thought the pen cap story was funny, and then stopped with a look of awe on his face when he saw the signature. "Who'd you get?" I looked at the inscription, which was very easy to read, and said, "Joe Morgan." Dad looked into the crowd to get a second glance at the player, "*That* was Joe Morgan?" He was star-struck. With my family having spent so much time in Ohio, specifically in the Cincinnati area during their college years, he was all too familiar with the great Reds players who played for The Big Red Machine. I had never seen my dad so thoroughly impressed by anyone. I would see this kind of amazement from my dad only once more in my lifetime, and that was also at a Cubs game. Lou Boudreau, the Hall of Fame player/manager for the Cleveland Indians, was the color commentator for WGN radio. We caught a glimpse of him after a game, and I thought Dad was going to run right into traffic to get to him. Through our trips to baseball games, I realized nobody is immune to the draw of celebrity; it simply takes the *right* celebrity to bring out the childlike awe. Years went by, and we continued to go out of our way to ask players to scrawl their names on cards. I occasionally tried to target the players I knew my father would be impressed with the most. To this day, I blame baseball for creating a thirst for celebrity encounters.

These days I don't go around hunting for autographs; primarily because I've been fortunate enough to successfully work in the entertainment industry, and have come to know more about the business and the difficulty of maintaining privacy and normalcy. Nowadays, I tend to look more for memories and photos than signatures. I don't generally track down a noteworthy person even if I know they're around. I will admit to occasionally having those *Holy Shit!* moments, much like my dad did all those years ago. Having a more nonchalant attitude towards the presence of the rich and famous, combined with my own skewed sense of humor and fun, has provided me with a host of stupid stories about famous people. I hope you enjoy them.

Audrey Hepburn

O f all of the celebrities I have had the pleasure of working with over the years, Audrey Hepburn would have to be *the* person I am asked about the most. It seemed only fitting I start this book with her. She was among the first big-name people I encountered, and she remains one of those people who inspires the most admiration. I only wish I had more to share with you.

Sometime between 1988 and 1990, while doing what I could to scrape together entertainment gigs and avoid living a life more ordinary, I found myself contacted by a performer and agent in the Chicago area who was not new to the business but was certainly new to me. Thankfully, my reputation as a reliable and high-quality performer was growing. Even better, my reputation was spreading. Fellow entertainers, as well as bookers who had used my services, were passing my name around, and it was generating more work. I had been given the name of this particular agent by a friend who had done a fair amount of work for him. After a few conversations and the obligatory mailing of my press kit, he called me for a very low-paying juggling show at a holiday festival, which I happily accepted. Having aced that show, the agent received many compliments from the end client, which in turn resulted in me receiving more phone calls for more low-paying gigs.

I had hoped I would get along with this agent better than I did. He too was a juggler, and we had many mutual friends. Unfortunately, I found myself taking work from him only to pad the wallet a little more — a *very* little more.

As a performer, his act was not particularly good. I saw lots of hackneyed material and plenty of things he never mastered before performing. I also didn't like the fact that he had only set up an agency so he could get more of the phone calls, not to build a business and reputation by booking others as well as himself. Many entertainers go this route. In and of itself, it's not a bad tactic; I myself worked as an agent/entertainer for many years, and it was a great thing. What was wrong with this particular person was his "I don't know how to do that, but I'll take it" attitude. This produced a poor product for the client, and adversely affected everyone else in the business; especially those he hired. If one juggler does a bad show for a lot of money, word spreads. Soon all jugglers are receiving fewer calls.

He also only called other acts for jobs with scant budgets, mark up the price so he made his full commission, and pay the talent poorly. I am not opposed to working lower-paying shows, but if I am expected to make less money, the agent should tighten the belt a little bit too.

The biggest pet peeve I had with him was how he would almost always call last-minute. I have preferred to work over not work. If I can take a job, even a last-minute one, I do my best to make everyone happy. When this agent called, the jobs rarely *didn't* require the performer to wear some sort of elaborate, themed costume or to offer special skills that were difficult to produce under such short notice. I cannot express how happy I was the day I knew I could refuse his phone calls without adversely affecting my bank account.

I'm not telling you this to "out" this agent. I lead with this background so you can fully appreciate how much I hate knowing it was this particular agent who booked me at the event where I had the pleasure to bask in the presence of the eternally beautiful Hollywood icon, Audrey Hepburn.

When he called about this gig, I had never been to the historic Palmer House Hotel in Chicago, nor did I have any idea the end client was UNICEF. I just knew this agent had called me and about five other variety performers, all *the* most-booked performers in the area, for the event. I was not only happy to be called for a gig where I could work with people whom I admired, but I was also amazed to see the paycheck. While nothing to retire on, this check was considerably larger than most of the ones I had earned from this guy in the past. Don't get crazy with your thoughts, I'm talking about $25 more than he usually booked me for, which by his standards was *considerably* larger.

Twenty-five bucks aside, the event did come with a typical annoying twist; he needed everyone to dress as a stereotypical French mime. Make-up, beret, gloves, the works. Given only one of the seven people booked for this show actually made his living as a mime, I feel confident in saying we didn't all have the necessary accoutrements. I know I didn't. After being assured we needed to be mimes in appearance only, I took the job. Luckily, I had plenty of make-up and a decent outfit which would pass muster. I also had a bit of actual mime training should the need to shut the hell up arise, all thanks to my time as a clown for Ringling Bros. and Barnum & Bailey Circus. Yes, I used to be a clown. Don't judge! I stopped taking gigs as a clown soon before this show, but always kept the equipment and costumes.

When I got to the Palmer House, I realized this was a black-tie, celebrity-filled affair. I also realized I certainly could have been paid more than a measly $25 extra, but my damn face was already covered in greasepaint, so I met up with everyone else and set about strolling the hotel ballrooms and entertaining the guests.

I learned that the event was a fundraiser for UNICEF, and that it featured the best of everything: world-class food, outstanding decor to match the *Parisian Nights* theme (Mimes, get it?), and plenty of television cameras and reporters scurrying about. As it happened, there were many local and national celebrities on-hand as well. Somehow, the only two I can recall were musician Buster Poindexter and the lovely Audrey Hepburn.

While I have never been one to get all squishy-giddy over celebrities, other than the sports heroes whose signatures I chased after as a kid, I admit that once I found out where I was and who was there, I got very excited to be a part of the show. I mean, Buster Poindexter had that song *Hot, Hot, Hot!* I'm kidding, of course. Audrey-*freaking* -Hepburn! I was excited just knowing she was there and occasionally seeing her flitting about the ballroom floor, and by the time I took my first break, I was ecstatic. I simply *had* to call my parents and share this particular bit of news with them. You see, no matter how successful you become as an entertainer, regardless of the level of notoriety you may personally achieve, I think all entertainers hope and pray their parents approve of their child's choice in profession. Tonight I was certain that telling my parents I was, in a small way, working with Audrey Hepburn would let them know I was, at the very least, a step up from being a birthday party clown.

With my break over, it was time to don the beret again and start juggling for the masses. Throughout the night, I caught glimpses of Miss Hepburn and hoped I would have an opportunity to meet her or at least shake her hand. However, at no point did I stray from my task of entertaining the crowd. I was being paid to be an entertainer, not to stalk one.

At one point, I had gathered a decent-sized crowd. In the midst of this particular crowd, I noticed Ms. Hepburn among the viewers offering applause and laughter. I smiled knowing she was in the audience. With Hollywood royalty watching, I felt this would be the closest to a command performance I'd ever get.

Towards the end of the evening, all of the performers were called by the event organizer to pose for photographs. I assumed these were just a few for some of the patrons and guests. I was not aware they would be photos with Hepburn herself. We all posed as various forms of faux French artiste-ness around Hepburn and a few other bigwig dignitary types. We had been instructed not to ask for autographs or individual photos with the legend, and to the best of my knowledge everyone simply went about their evening. I had another scheduled break coming up, so I went to a nearby drinking fountain near the elevator to relax.

I couldn't help but stare as Hepburn strolled through the room. She was simply beautiful, elegant, and poised; everything you hoped someone of her stature would be. I quietly marveled at how she graciously suffered every fool gladly after our photo opportunity. So many people approached her hoping to shake her hand or get a few moments with her. I didn't see her turn anyone away.

I would love to be able to tell you I had a moment like the many who approached her after our photographs were taken. I would give anything to say I shook her hand and chatted with her, even though I am certain I would have offered nothing of interest to this woman of the world. I *can* say that I was close enough to her to know that she smelled lovely and radiated elegance. I've always said I was within spitting distance of her, and for me that was more than good enough. I can also say, while I do not have a photograph with her or her signature on a napkin, I did have a genuine moment with her; one that I will cherish forever. Even better, I had something cool I could tell my parents once the gig was over.

After the last of the autograph-seekers and fans left, she turned and made her way toward me and the elevator. I had a juggling prop in my hand and was about to make my way back into the crowd for one last pass. I saw her and muttered something silly like, "Back to work I go!" She smiled that perfect Hollywood smile at me, and our eyes met. This was it. This was *my* opportunity, and likely my only chance to ever really say anything to her. Not wanting to fawn over her like so many had that night, and not wanting to do anything other than make her smile again, I said something to her as she walked past me. Something designed to be silly but memorable. Maybe even awkwardly charming and reverent.

"Miss Hepburn," I said. "You're one classy broad."
She stopped, looked back at me, smiled her famous smile and replied, "Darling, you have no idea!"

With that, she walked away, full of grace and beauty. Like a scene from a movie, she got on the elevator and turned just as the doors closed. I thought she was one amazing person before, but at that moment I knew she was damned cool as well.

To this day I have never seen a single image from this event. I did manage to see myself, and others, on the Chicago news juggling and entertaining. One time, I was even in the frame with her; my only on-screen appearance with her. I still hold out hope that I will find or be sent a copy or two of the photos we took together. Until then, I love to think about the night where an agent I hated brought me face-to-face with a performer everyone loved.

If you're curious, mom and dad were indeed impressed and wanted to hear more when I got home. Dad was particularly moved when he heard I was in the presence of greatness. I knew he would at least perk up a little bit. He'd mentioned Miss Hepburn many times in the past as one of the most beautiful and graceful actresses ever, although it was mom who had let out a little squeal of excitement while on the phone with me. They both expressed their happiness and told me they were proud. No performer can ask for more.

CHAPTER THREE

John Glenn,

C. Everett Coop, and

Ted Kennedy

I graduated high school in 1988. Like most kids, I was expected to venture off to college. My father was a high school teacher for over 25 years, and taught at the collegiate level at one point. You can imagine the pressure on his child to go to an institute of higher learning. I did indeed have my heart set on attending school after graduating from Marengo Community High School, however my father was not particularly happy with my college of choice.

I had set my sights on Ringling Bros. and Barnum & Bailey Clown College. I'd known since I was ten that I wanted to be in the entertainment field, so I decided I would either go to a university with an acclaimed track record for fostering the performing arts, or I would gain knowledge from places like Chicago's Second City or Ringling Bros. From there, I would learn even more from the countless failed auditions and whatever skills I could acquire from actual time on stage. I knew my family could never afford any of the universities and colleges I hoped to attend, and frankly, my test scores probably wouldn't have gotten me in anywhere anyway. Therefore, Clown College seemed like the perfect place to go.

I first learned about RBBBCC several years earlier when, out of nowhere, a brochure arrived in our mailbox. I have no idea if I was on some sort of mailing list thanks to my subscription to *Juggler's World* magazine or not. I only knew this looked like a good school for me. As I was entering local talent contests and beginning to take on work juggling for local events, I often mentioned to my parents that Ringling Bros. was my school of choice. This rarely sat well with dad. Really, I couldn't blame him. Ringling Bros. is not exactly Columbia.

There was a television special about the institution of higher hilarity on CBS for the 20th anniversary of the Clown College hosted by Dick Van Dyke. The show featured a few of the comedians I had seen on numerous television shows such as Johnny Carson's *Tonight Show*. I recorded the special and watched it many times with my parents. Dad started to come around when he saw the rigorous amount of training each student received. This may have been funny business, but it was no joke. I think what put him over the edge was learning RBBBCC was statistically harder to get into than Harvard Medical School. With upwards of 3,000 to 4,000 applicants every year and annual class sizes being around 50 or 60 students, he realized just getting in was something of a Herculean feat.

Shortly before my high school graduation, I got word that the Ringling folks were holding auditions in Chicago. I *had* to go. I had no idea how well I did throughout the process, I simply hoped my skills, experience, attitude, and answers to the ten-page application would get me in. Sometime that summer I received my acceptance, and was off to Venice, Florida for nearly eleven weeks of intense training. Even though my parents were supportive and came to the commencement show and ceremony, I was never quite certain they thought I was making a good decision with my career. A few gigs locally, an appearance or two on WGN TV's *The Bozo Show*, and one phone call from Ringling Bros. later, I believed they would certainly realize it was a good life choice.

It was not uncommon for the Ringling Bros. office to receive requests for performers at high-profile corporate events across the country. I, however, was unaware of this until I received a call in early 1989 from Ruth Chaddock of the Clown College asking if I was available for a date in Washington, D.C. I asked what the event was, and she told me it was for the Washington Press Club's celebration of the 101st Congress. The theme was *The Political Circus*, and as the Ringling headquarters were also in D.C., it was natural to have us there. This wasn't the awesome Press Corps annual dinner, affectionately known as the Nerd Prom. No, I like to think this more like the area press making a peace offering and saying "thank you" to the politicians for allowing them to ruin their political lives during the previous year. The guest list consisted of elected officials, many big name celebrities, and, very likely, the newly inaugurated President, George H. W. Bush. I couldn't believe the news, and I was all too eager to tell my parents that their 19-year old son was going to be performing for the President.

As far as I was concerned, this was more of a paid vacation than anything else. I had never been to D.C., and we had some time packaged in around the show date which allowed for sightseeing and other fun. Plus, I was making a decent paycheck for the event. It was a great time to be 19 and struggling to find an identity in entertainment. Even if this identity was covered in greasepaint, it was a good gig. My parents wanted me to check in whenever possible with general happenings, politician sightings, and if I was having fun.

As far as corporate events go, this one was great. We all went through some basic security checks and training in case the President was in attendance, and we were all given specific stations within the hotel to do our clown-covered tasks. In my opinion, I had the best job of the night.

The party guests had to enter the hotel and head down an escalator to the banquet hall. One clown was at the door and I was at the escalator. We were essentially brightly covered "This way, Dummy" signs. Essentially, I got to see the attendees before any of the press downstairs. It was very cool.

I had never expected to meet the likes of newsman Garrick Utley, actress Lauren Hutton, and White House

Chief of Staff John Sununu. I certainly never expected to meet these people while cracking wise in full clown regalia, and it was a little overwhelming. I watched guest after guest enter the building and began wondering how many political decisions were made at affairs like this. I pondered which of these people may or may not have received a vote or a criticism from my parents, and how many of them were escorted by someone other than their wives; I saw a *lot* of old, white-haired gentlemen with very young, gorgeous women in evening gowns.

Not being very politically-minded at the time, I struggled to see anyone I could identify. I recognized Senator John Glenn immediately for a couple of reasons, neither of which had to do with politics. First, my parents never stopped making us aware of every damn famous person Ohio ever produced. They were both from the Buckeye State, and never lost a bit of pride about it. Seriously, I cannot tell you how many times they mentioned a politician, sports figure, author, inventor, or entertainer in casual conversation because they were from Ohio. Second, I'm geek! John Glenn was the first damned American man to orbit the Earth for God's sake! There was a Mercury astronaut right in front of me! How the hell did I get lucky enough to be in the same room with John Glenn, much less shake his hand?

I had no choice but to remain in character and keep the light-hearted hilarity flowing in the room. As he approached the escalator I kept shaking in my oversized shoes. John f'ing Glenn was heading my way. I'm certain he was walking in slow motion, and the music from *The Right Stuff* was playing in the background, but in reality none of that happened. He made it to the escalator, and I introduced myself. He smiled and humored me. Thinking about my parents and how elated they would be to hear I met John Glenn, I greeted him as "A nice Ohio boy" which prompted him to ask if I was from Ohio. I told him about my parents and their admiration of him. I took the opportunity to make a joke before sending him down to the banquet. "So . . . what have you done with yourself since orbiting the Earth? Anything good?" He laughed and said, "Well, I am a U.S. Senator." I smiled and said, "So, nothing? Ah, well, we still love you. Since you've already come down so far, go a little further down these stairs and follow the signs." Glenn laughed, shook my hand again, and wished me a good night.

As the evening progressed, and the list of politicians and celebrities grew, I rarely took notice. I had no choice but to stop everything I was doing, however, when one specific gentleman entered the room. Seriously, I had no choice. Quite literally, *everyone* in the room stopped and looked in reverence when Surgeon General C. Everett Coop walked in. Maybe it was the uniform and the epaulets that brought such genuine awe from the crowd. Perhaps, it was how well he served as the Surgeon General and how respected he was that caused the room to stop and watch as if royalty had entered the room. I like to think it was simply because nobody back then was rocking such a high-quality man-beard and he looked badass!

It was rather impressive to see anyone walk into a respect-filled room. In 1989, we had just begun the Rush Limbaugh era where friends of different political backgrounds were supposed to stop being friends. By today's standards, nobody would get such treatment from anyone in this country. It really is shameful to think I can look back to the end of the 80s as a time where things were more civil and polite.

As Coop approached me, I made a point of shaking his hand and addressed him as General Coop. We chatted a bit, and I hoped to change his oft-stern countenance into a smile. Being a clown representing Ringling Bros., there were plenty of things I shouldn't or couldn't say, but the comedian in me couldn't resist saying to the man best known for changing the country with his anti-tobacco stance, "I bet you are *dying* for a cigarette. Head downstairs. Watch out for the photographers." Everyone around him busted out laughing, and Coop did his very best to keep his smirk from turning into a full-blown smile. I won the day and he laughed and patted me on the shoulder before heading downstairs.

The highlight of the evening came soon after Coop made his exit down the escalator. If John Glenn represented everything my geeky heart stood for, and C. Everett Coop was the walking embodiment of respect, it seemed actual royalty was about to head my way. At least by U.S. standards.

I don't care who you are or what your political affiliation may be. It doesn't matter if you follow politics religiously or care nothing for it at all. If you were around any time between 1960 and 2009, you would recognize a Kennedy if you saw one. Especially Ted Kennedy, the last real link to the Camelot days of the United States. As far as I was concerned, the night was going to produce no bigger star even if the President himself showed up. A Kennedy entering the room is a big deal. Not that you would have known by watching the crowd.

While Coop got the royal treatment, Kennedy was barely noticed. A few of his friends were on-hand to shake his hand and make small talk, but nobody else acknowledged his presence. Perhaps it was because he was not being his overly charming, up for reelection self. Personally, I think it was because he was such a fixture in Washington that his presence was no longer something that inspired awe. I suppose, it would've been more shocking if Kennedy hadn't arrived for such an event. Where his was going to be *the* name I would remember most, and surely the one my parents would be most impressed to hear, he wasn't headed anywhere near me or the party.

I had been told not to leave my post for any reason. However, I was *not* going to miss a chance to shake a Kennedy's hand. Andy the Clown walked towards him, and I can only imagine what he was thinking to see an orange-haired freak in makeup bounding his way. Lord knows how many times he had seen such an apparition in his head over the years, but this time it was *real*. Mysteriously, nobody stopped me from getting close to the senator.

When he was closer to me he looked me squarely in the eyes and laughed. "Mr. Vice President," he said, "How nice to see you!" Poor Dan Quayle. He had no idea how many times I had heard the same joke that evening. I shook his hand, and told him what an honor it was to meet him. I took his arm and escorted him towards the escalator. For the life of me I can't remember a damned thing I said to him. I can only assume it was mindless blather about the event, the hotel, and how cool it was to be talking to him. I was definitely freaking out a bit to be walking arm-in-arm with a Kennedy. It would seem I was the only one who cared. I do remember thinking, "Why the hell am I standing here covered head-to-toe in fucking clown crap on the day I get to meet someone like him?" I felt a bit embarrassed, but I remained in character and did my job well. While I wish I could remember more of our conversation, one odd thing did stand out. Sweet Mother of God! He had the *largest* head I had ever seen on a human being. It was as though he were a life-sized bobble-head caricature of himself, only his head was easily twice the exaggerated size you'd find on many of the figurines at a sports collectables shop. I half expected John Glenn to come back upstairs, circle around Kennedy's noggin, and then return downstairs. He was glassy-eyed, his complexion very red. His hair was disheveled, and he didn't have what my dad called the "election season look" –Kennedy would trim down for the cameras when he was up for reelection. His current appearance was a little off-putting, but hey, when you meet a Kennedy, you take what you can get.

I can't remember attempting to make any jokes with him, but I do recall him being quite charming and polite. Then again, how can you be rude to a clown in front of a bunch of reporters? It was Kennedy himself who provided the line of the night, and the defining moment of my encounter with him. As I led him towards the escalator, I gave him a brief rundown of where everything was. We made it to the top of the moving staircase, shook hands one last time, and asked him if there was anything at all I could do for him. He thanked me for my time, looked me up and down and then with a wobble of his unusually large head asked, "Er . . . uh . . . where's the baahr?" I was more than happy to give him directions to the nearest bar and sent him on his way.

For the record, that was my parents' favorite story of the night.

CHAPTER FIVE

Meadowlark Lemon
and Curly Neal

I t is not at all uncommon for major companies to sponsor shows, concerts, theatrical productions, and sporting events. In fact, many times I've met and/or worked with someone of note under the auspices of a big box store or a corporation showcasing their products. That was certainly the case with the annual company picnic for Sears, who sponsored racing legend, A.J. Foyt, and music superstar, Phil Collins. While I don't have any stupid stories about either of them, I enjoyed getting paid to watch a concert by Phil Collins, and I loved watching Foyt start his Indy car inside the convention hall because someone in the crowd insisted it was a phony display car and not the real deal. I think the sound of that engine revving in an enclosed space scared the hell out of every man, woman, and child in the Chicago suburbs.

I was booked to perform some strolling juggling in the housewares department of Sears at the Woodfield Mall in Schaumburg, Illinois. They were having a family weekend, and wanted the entire store filled with activities for all ages. Harlem Globetrotters legend, Meadowlark Lemon, was one of the celebrities appearing at the event. This confused me. Sears wasn't sponsoring the Globetrotters that year, and Lemon had long severed ties with the Globetrotter organization in order to promote his short-lived Bucketeers franchise. Nevertheless, there he was in the sporting goods department signing basketballs, photos, and damn near anything anyone handed him.

It was quite a thrill for me to see him. In my mind he, along with the rest of the Globetrotters from his era, was about the biggest celebrity on the planet. Many people forget the Globetrotter years when Geese Ausbie, Meadowlark Lemon, and Curly Neal were mainstays on *ABC's Wide World of Sports*. Does anyone else remember their ridiculous Saturday morning cartoon series where they all turned into bizarre superheroes? I never missed a game or that awful series on television, and was fortunate enough to see them live with my dad and my brother on a few occasions.

Thankfully, I always arrive early to my events, and was able to stand in line to grab a signed photograph of him. Unfortunately, that was about all I managed to get out of the experience, even though there weren't a ton of people there. I was shuffled in and out of line rather quickly, and he wasn't particularly engaging with the crowd. I couldn't tell if he was tired or simply unfazed by the entire thing. I am certain he had done countless such appearances during his career. Perhaps there was some bad blood between him and the team, and he disliked signing images of himself in Globetrotters attire. I only know that on that particular day, he didn't shake a lot of hands, answer too many questions, or make a whole lot of kids smile during his appearance. I left the table, tucked away my photo, and went on to perform my gig. I confess I was a little sad to see one of my idols acting apathetic around his fans. But, hey, everyone has bad days. It definitely wasn't the Globetrotter experience of my dreams. The experience of my dreams happened several years before that, and featured my favorite member of the team, Curly Neal.

I was around 18 when I was booked to perform at the Food Marketing Institute's trade show at McCormick Place in Chicago. Ringling Bros. had contacted me on behalf of Procter and Gamble who had a booth at the event and was sponsoring the circus in several different markets across the country. This was a great chance to do a little cross-promoting. It was also a well-paying gig at the time for a single day's worth of shaking hands, posing for photos, and attracting attention to the Procter and Gamble booth. As it happened, P & G was also sponsoring the Harlem Globetrotters. Meeting *any* of the legendary Harlem Globetrotters was cool, but for a comedian and juggler like me, the fast-dribbling, ball-spinning, basketball acrobat, Curly Neal was the guy to meet. He was also the first celebrity I met in full clown regalia.

My job description was pretty straightforward: as a circus clown, attract attention to the booth in order to bring more potential business to the client; which is really the *only* reason an entertainer is hired to work a trade show booth.

Aside from generally being a clown, I handed out Ringling Bros. souvenirs, coupons and fliers for Procter and Gamble products, and gave away free samples of Puritan Oil in new shatterproof plastic bottles. I juggled said bottles and anything else I could get my hands on.

It was a fun event for me. At the time, I had limited experience at trade shows and I remember enjoying most everything about the experience. I also had no real appreciation for just how massive the grocery industry was. The show itself was enormous, and there were a lot of stars on-hand doing exactly the same thing I was. I even bumped into country music legend Kenny Rogers while roaming the convention floor. Unfortunately, I don't have a stupid story about Kenny Rogers, so he doesn't get his own chapter. If it makes you feel any better, Rogers was the first big name to hear me utter the phrase, "Hey, has anyone ever told you, you look a lot like (insert name here)?" From Cyndi Lauper to Dee Snider, and even Rogers himself, the standard reply is always, "I get that a lot."

It doesn't matter how big a star you are, if a big company sponsored your musical act, touring show, or television program, it was very likely you would appear at a booth posing for photographs to bring in more people. I learned very quickly that no matter how famous you become as an entertainer, you will never outgrow the need to work a corporate event. The only real difference is seen on the paycheck.

I attracted my crowds, juggled my bottles, gave away gallons of Puritan Oil in shatterproof containers, and told everyone to check out the circus on specific dates. I also made certain to tell everyone to come back for the next two days so they could meet the one and only Curly Neal. This energy and professionalism made an impact with the folks who hired me. At the end of the day I was asked, "Is there any way we could get you to come back for the rest of the show? You're doing a great job." I was extremely excited. Not only was I going to add two extra days of pay to my wallet, but now I was going to meet Curly Neal!

The next day was the same song, but different verse. Mr. Neal was set to appear by 11 am. Like a kid at the end of a school day I watched the clock with anticipation. When he finally arrived, the entire place erupted with energy. He looked amazing, as if not a single day had passed from his playing days. That big smile and extreme personality filled the booth and much of the convention floor. People were lined up to see him.

Not wanting to overstep my bounds, I made certain to steer clear of his signing area and not act like the star-struck ten-year-old kid who was in my brain at that moment. Turns out, I had no reason to worry about it. He couldn't wait to meet the dude in the clown makeup. He joked with me about the business, asked me about my life, and was generally a fun man to be around. At one point he said, "You've got it easy, kid." I asked what he meant, and he replied, "I had to be a clown too, but if I wasn't funny, they knew exactly which fool to hate. You can take off that makeup and nobody knows if you were the guy who wasn't funny!"

After the requisite telling of tales regarding my admiration for him and all he had accomplished, he went about his day signing autographs and posing for pictures. There was not a soul in the room who did not get truly memorable one-on-one time with Neal. During slower times, he would walk over to me and watch me juggling and interacting with the crowd, laughing at my jokes and taking a real interest in the many different juggling props I had in my bag.

It was no surprise to me to hear that Neal could juggle. Watching him with a basketball on the court showed he was extremely dexterous and skilled at manipulating objects with ease. What was surprising, was that he wasn't particularly good at it and was hoping I could give him some pointers. That was a trip! Me, an 18-year-old kid in clown makeup teaching one of the single most skilled sets of hands how to improve his juggling skills? No. Freaking. Way! Aside from being all too eager to try out everything I had with me and learn more tricks, he was interested in ways he could apply those skills with a basketball. Even though he was not performing much anymore, he was always staying in shape and making appearances, either on behalf of the Globetrotters or as a business partner with a relatively new NBA franchise, the Orlando Magic. He told me, "You are never too old to learn a new trick."

Throughout the day, we spoke about the Globetrotters origins in Illinois (Google it!), life on the road, our families, and anything two new friends could discuss. We shared lunch, he often insisted we pose for photos together, and he made me feel as important in that booth as he was. This was a very classy gentleman. I really couldn't have asked for three better days of employment, even if I was relegated to being the mystery man under the wig and makeup.

The crowning moment for me, and one which still stands out as a dream-come-true highlight, was when the P&G booth would play the familiar "Sweet Georgia Brown" intermittently throughout the day. The company had two Globetrotter basketballs there that were to be signed by Neal and raffled off to convention guests at the end of the show. Almost any time the music started playing, and that iconic whistle would echo through the airwaves, Neal would smile brightly, grab a basketball and showcase his incredible ball-handling skills. Wearing a fancy three-piece suit didn't hinder him from displaying absolute magic with the ball and everybody screamed and cheered with absolute appreciation. He would find young ladies with kids and get the ball to spin on the children's fingers. He was every bit the showman in that booth as he was on the court.

As if seeing a demonstration like that in person wasn't enough for me, he would frequently call out to me to toss the ball around with him. After seeing me juggle and showing him a few things, he would insist I come out with him and do a few tricks of my own. While I claim no masterful skill compared to his, I did generate a lot of applause and laughs with every exchange. As far as I was concerned, I was tossing the ball around in the Magic Circle with one of the greats. Life goal, *achieved!* I remember shaking his hand and telling him he made a dream come true for me and he just laughed and said, "Get more rest, kid. You need more dreams!"

By the time the show was over, we had spent several hours laughing, selling Proctor and Gamble products, and having a great time. I know there are photographs out there featuring me and Neal. Perhaps someday, someone will locate an odd pic of Curly Neal, a clown, and several bottles of Puritan Oil and send it to me. Until then, I remain truly grateful for the fun Neal – and all of the Globetrotters –have brought to my life.

That sounds like a joke. "Curly Neal, a circus clown, and a bottle of vegetable oil walk into a bar. . ."

CHAPTER SIX

Bozo, Wizzo, and Cooky

During my time in Chicago, I appeared on some version of *The Bozo Show* a total of six times. Bozo was, and remains, one of the biggest Chicago area celebrities. The show ran on WGN TV for just shy of 40 years in one form or another. You could tune in daily to watch *Bozo's Circus*, or weekly to see the *Bozo Super Sunday Show*. During the holiday season, you could enjoy watching *Bozo's Grand March for Kids*. In its day, it was one of the most watched television programs around. Originally broadcast live, it featured crazy comedy sketches, music, and talented circus acts from around the world. In many ways, it was the Ed Sullivan Show for kids. By the time cable television came along, WGN was the first superstation. People with basic cable anywhere in the Western Hemisphere could watch Cubs baseball and pre-taped episodes of *Bozo*. The show was so popular, there was a minimum five-year waiting list to get tickets, and it became a well-paying *gas gig* for acts who came to town, or passed through, during their regularly scheduled tour schedules.

WGN simply owned kids programming, and was something of a magical television station with shows like *The Bozo Show*, *Garfield Goose and Friends*, and my personal favorite, *The Ray Rayner Show*. I still believe watching Ray Rayner march around the studio with Chelveston the Duck is damn near as close to perfection as television has or ever will get with regard to entertainment value and pure simplicity. Look it up. I occasionally missed my school bus waiting to see him parade around with that damned duck!

During its 40-year run, two people played the internationally known clown. The first, and arguably the more famous, was Bob Bell. Bell, along with Roy Brown as Cooky the Clown, Marshall Brodien as Wizzo the Wizard, and Frazier Thomas with his pal, Garfield Goose, captivated kids with their pie fights, crazy voices, and the always impressive array of games for kids and adults. I remember watching moms versus dads in a pillowcase changing race, kids versus their parents racing eggs on spoons across the stage, and of course the all-time favorite Grand Prize Game also known as Bozo Buckets. I cannot tell you how many times I would agonize watching kids, randomly chosen by the impossibly low-tech Bozo-puter, attempt to toss a ping pong ball into that sixth bucket hoping to win all of the prizes they had accrued so far, and achieve the ultimate glory for any kid: a fifty-dollar bill and a brand new Schwinn bicycle. It's hard to imagine now, but any kid who got past the fourth bucket generated so much tension and excitement for a television audience, that nails were bitten clean off hands around the country. A ping pong ball, a bucket, a kid, a clown, and a prize. That's all you needed to make compelling television.

When Bob Bell retired, the show was revamped somewhat and the role of Bozo was taken over by actor Joey D'Auria. Brown remained as Cooky for several years and Brodien kept using the Stone of Zanzibar to create his special brand of magic for kids. The regular antics of comedy, fun, and games accompanied by cartoons continued. Since then, there had been many cast

members on the show, including a bizarre stint with actor, Adrian Zmed. I'll let you do all the Googling you
want about the Bozo cast at your leisure.

My first time with the Bozo gang was actually a very
inauspicious and frustrating affair. This was about
1988, and I was doing a favor for a local casting director
by donating my time to perform on one of the many
stages at of a large fundraiser called *Bozo's Grand
March for Kids* scheduled at the Rosemont Horizon (now
the Allstate Arena) where toys, clothing, food, and more
were being donated to help area children. Everything
about this event was a catastrophe. Nobody could direct
me to where I was supposed to work. At one point I was
shuttled into a corner, told to wait, and summarily for-
gotten about. Parking was a disaster, the sound was
overbearing, and nobody knew where anything was supposed to happen. I got fed up and figured this free show
was over. Especially since, I'd only accepted the event
because it was supposed to be televised, and any Bozo
gig in Chicago was good for business.

In 1989, I received a call from WGN TV directly.
They somehow remembered me from the previous year's
debacle, and wanted to make amends by guaranteeing
me a spot on their next, "more organized", charity show.
I am certain by more "organized", they meant "still
crazy, and a hell of a lot colder" since this event was held

in December in the parking lot of the WGN television studios, and all of the stage shows were outside. In my career, I've juggled in all kinds of weather conditions. I honestly don't remember having more frigid, frozen fingers in my life. I was stuck outside for hours waiting to perform a fifteen-minute show for a bunch of crazed children waiting to see Bozo and get free toys. However, true to their word, I was in the finished product which aired on the superstation. Everyone in my family was thrilled with the show, and I set about promoting myself to area agents and organizations, which was always the main impetus for me to do the show. Every time that program aired, an estimated 25 million people across the country saw it, I would get fresh video to use when selling the act, and I had a perfect opportunity to market to agents across the United States. Hell, people in Costa Rica saw me on *The Bozo Show.*

After that initial appearance, I frequently received phone calls from long-time producer, Allen Hall, asking if I had something new for the show. Not for their holiday special, but for *the* show, which was considerably more fun for me. For one, the show was filmed *inside*, with perfect lighting, great cameras, a captive studio audience, and the crew was always stellar to work with. For another, the kid in me actually got to hang around with Bozo and Cooky, both in and out of makeup. That was pretty damn cool, and I always felt a little guilty for being there. I remember only one time where WGN had caught up to the waiting list for tickets, and when they re-opened the opportunity to request tickets to the show, the list filled up to over a five-year wait almost immediately. Here I was at a show people were willing to wait years to see, and I just waltzed right on in. It was a little too much for me to think about the first time out.

I never did see D'Auria off set, but on set he was a delight to work with. He was always quick to remember my previous appearances on the show, and took great care with information and name pronunciation when introducing my act. He watched every minute of every segment I did for the show, and made certain the kids in the crowd were cheering all the way. I had seen his real life persona in a play once, and I made a point of telling him (backstage of course) how much I liked his work with or without the bozo wig. He was always mindful of where he was, and never once broke character around the kids. Joey D'Auria was a great Bozo who carried on the legacy well.

I had the pleasure of working with magician Marshall Brodien many times in my career before working with him on television. I have known more magicians in my career than most people, and I have yet to find a single

person who has a bad thing to say about Marshall Brodien. Kids loved him. Parents loved him. The world
loved him.

My favorite person to work with on the show was Roy
Brown. In many ways, he was the binding force that held
the show together during the transition from Bob Bell
to Joey D'Auria. The first time I met him, he was out of
makeup for a show rehearsal. Later that day, in full
makeup, I admit I got a little star-struck. When I rein-
troduced myself to Cooky, he smiled and reminded me
that we had already met. I told him, "I know, but the
seven-year-old me has always wanted to meet Cooky."
He shook my hand, and acted like I had crushed it. In
Cooky's voice, he said, "Can't be *that* nice to meet me.
That huuuuurt!"

Roy Brown was always quick to crack wise on or off
stage, and watching him and Allen Hall discuss the old
days of the show was like watching a classic bit of television in its own right. In the circus business, the telling
of circus tales is called *shooting jackpots.* These two
were always shooting jackpots, filling the room with
funny stories and animated reenactments of when things
didn't go right during the live television days. I fully admit I cried like a baby when I heard Roy Brown died. He
was a great man.

You've clearly seen there were no ridiculous one-liners produced from any interactions with these classic characters. I loved every time I was on *The Bozo Show.* Everyone treated me with great kindness, and I always welcomed another opportunity to perform on the show. Many times after I had performed my plate-spinning routine on the show, if there wasn't a guest lined up, they would edit in my performance. One time, I called Allen Hall and told him, "You can just call me any time. I'll always have something for you." He replied, "Yeah, but I love that damn plate act!" They must have shown me spinning plates on that show fifty times. At least, that's how many times I was woken up early on a Sunday morning by friends who were watching that segment on the show. Yes, my adult friends watched Bozo on Sunday mornings. You got a problem with that?

Regardless of how much fun it was to be a very small part of this historic television show, I should address one thing people always ask me about, which includes a stupid confession. I mentioned that the show used to be a very good way for entertainers to make money. Well, by the time I was on the show, those days were long gone, and acts did the show in exchange for promotional consideration instead. This meant I could use the footage to promote myself without the fear of being sued by WGN, but I wasn't getting paid to perform. I'm quite certain one of the main reasons they liked booking me was that I was a high-quality act willing to do the show for free. Over the years, as the quality of the comedy writing dwindled, so did the quality of the acts appearing on the show. I felt it was still a good show to do, and I was always honored when they asked me back. Still, a guy should get something for his time other than a few memories and a videotape, right?

Knowing I would not be paid for the shows, I chose a little souvenir from each appearance. This is a very polite way of saying I stole something from the Bozo set every time I performed. It was never anything big, expensive, or irreplaceable. I'm not a jerk! No, they were very simple things that only meant something to me, and generally they were items only I knew were from the show. Most often, I took a ping pong ball from the Grand Prize Game. One time, it was a *Bozo Super Sunday Show* cast button, I took right off of Bozo's costume. I walked right up to Bozo during rehearsal, dusted off his shoulders, and took the pin. He laughed and asked if I was going to sell it online. For the record, I never sold any of the items I liberated from WGN TV, however, I no longer own any of them.

The ping pong balls were used in my act whenever I performed at a school or park district event. When some starry-eyed kid who worshipped Bozo came up to me to ask questions about their clown hero, I would give away one of the ping pong balls and tell them where it came from. The cast button also went to a kid from one of my audiences who had seen many of my performances on the show and was not only a fan of Bozo, but of me. My favorite item from the set, and one which I truly wish I still had, was a Polaroid photograph of Roy Brown in civilian clothing, holding a bottle of alcohol and sitting next to a cardboard cutout of his clown counterpart.

The first time I was actually on set, I had been asked to arrive very early for rehearsals, sound checks, camera positioning, and the like. The kind of early I still can't believe exists. We're talking, no traffic on the Kennedy Expressway early. When I wasn't needed for a rehearsal segment, I would wait in the green room or hang out on set to watch how this incarnation of one of television's most beloved shows was created. While backstage, I noticed the photograph, and my tradition of stealing something from the Bozo set was born. I kept that picture on my bulletin board for a very long time, and showed it to anyone who asked me about my time on the show. That photo was priceless, and my only real treasured possession. Unfortunately, it was confiscated by a girl after she broke up with me who threw it away.

I now wish I had kept one of those ping pong balls, however, I still have all the tapes and some of the appearances live on YouTube today. I may not be famous, and I may not have ever been on Johnny Carson, but I *was* on *The Bozo Show.*

CHAPTER SEVEN

Garfield Goose

For those of you not from the Chicago area or the Midwest, *Garfield Goose and Friends* appeared on television from 1952 to 1976. The simple, charming puppet was the brainchild of Frazier Thomas – who created the character as a way to raise donations for a children's charity. If you lived in the Chicago area, and watched WGN TV religiously, you would know that puppets like Cuddly Duddly and Garfield Goose were *kings* of the airwaves. In fact, Garfield Goose was quite literally a king; the self-proclaimed King of the United States, sporting a crown and everything.

The puppet was originally operated by Bruce Newton, who was not allowed to speak due to the union rules of television and radio at the time. Eventually, Newton was replaced by Roy Brown – the same Roy Brown who went on to portray the beloved Cooky the Clown mentioned in the previous chapter. Thomas first brought the beloved character to the airwaves in Cincinnati before heading out to Chicago where the show would find a home on WBKB, WBBM, and WGN. The Garfield Goose program was the longest-running puppet television show in history.

In the years after the program went off the air, Bruce Newton and his wife, Claire, went on to produce live events with the beloved Goose. There has always been a dispute over who created this character, but most agree Thomas was the man behind the Goose and not Newton. While there was some controversy surrounding the Newton's appearances, WGN chose not to pursue legal action against them. For many years after his lengthy run on television, the only way you could see Garfield Goose was at a fair, city festival, or school show. In fact, a small town festival is where I first met the Newtons and Garfield.

That first time I opened for them, they were so taken with my performance they made certain to get my contact information. Yes, I opened for a puppet, but I had the bigger dressing room. I received a lovely hand-drawn cartoon card of Garfield Goose from the Newtons thanking me for being such a great guy to work with, and I kept that card for many years. I had the honor of working with them quite a few times over the years, and they referred me to quite a few people.

Claire was always quick to dispense hugs to anyone she met, and even though she had the appearance of an overly made up grandparent, the hugs were always happily returned by the kids in attendance . . . and me. I admit, I was afraid to hug Claire because she seemed so brittle for such a vibrant and active person, and I swear I heard her creak every time I had hugged her. Nevertheless, she would hug with all her might and wouldn't take no for an answer.

She and Bruce made over 150 live appearances a year at festivals, schools, and just about any event for children. Over the years, more and more adults would stare in awe instead of the children they brought to meet the legend. Their shows featured music, juggling, bad jokes, and of course, other puppets from the television show. Few could get people's faces to come alive like Garfield Goose.

When I was still dating my now ex-wife, April, she would occasionally accompany me to the various events

I worked. Any chance to ride a carnival ride or eat a funnel cake was a good excuse to enjoy a Saturday in Chicago. On one such occasion, she came along as I performed at what could only be described as a lame little festival; a gig I did to fill in time and make a little extra cash. There weren't a lot of attractions worth getting out of the car for, but she found a sunny patch to read in and decided to wait out my performance rather than try to have any fun there.

As I finished up my performance and was getting ready to exit the grounds, I noticed Bruce and Claire setting up their stage. I hadn't seen them in many years, and was happy to see they were still working. After a "remember me?" greeting and several bone-creaking hugs from Claire, I went to the car to pack my gear. I jokingly asked April if she wanted to meet one of my celebrity friends. To be honest, I figured she was too cool or too young to even know who the hell Garfield Goose was. When she asked who at this sad little festival might be considered remotely famous (gee, thanks) I told her Garfield Goose was in attendance. She sprang up from her seat eager to meet the King himself. I couldn't believe how happy she was.

I introduced her to Bruce and Claire, who pounced with big hugs all around, and we chatted away like old friends. Before long, I asked Bruce if April could meet

Garfield. I expected him to bring out the puppet and have a few stories for her, let her touch the thing, and that would be that. Instead, Bruce let her *meet* Garfield. There he was, beak, crown, and all, "alive" and carrying on a conversation with my fully grown adult girlfriend. Given that Garfield didn't speak, other than the clacking sound of his puppet beak, Claire and Bruce carried on as if April had stepped into a routine from the TV show. I could not stop smiling watching her interact with this senior citizen with a sock puppet goose on his forearm. April asked if it was OK to hug Garfield. Indeed, it was A-OK with His Royal Highness. Soon afterwards, we said our goodbyes and April smiled the whole way home.

Later, she confessed she was a little embarrassed. "I just hugged a man's arm". I told her she hugged Garfield Goose, and that got rid of the embarrassment. April mentioned that she was certain when she hugged Claire she heard a crackling sound. I just laughed.

To this day, April still talks about that show. Even though we're no longer married, we stay in touch. She has told me many times that of all the things we've done together and of all the people I've introduced her to, meeting Garfield Goose is among the most impressive. I am hesitant to disagree with her. I know for certain that she wasn't the only adult that day to hug that silly old

Goose. For many people in the Chicagoland area, he represented everything that was good and pure in the world.

That was the last time I saw either of the Newtons. Claire passed away in July 2006 at the age of 78. I have no idea if Bruce is still alive or if he continued to perform. Hearing of her passing, I couldn't stop thinking about that day and all the other times we worked together. I remember the hand-drawn Garfield Goose card from our very first meeting, an item which has sadly been lost to the many moves I have made across the country. They were always so kind and so generous with their time. I loved and admired the way something as simple as a puppet who never uttered a word, could captivate and charm children of any age. In retrospect, I really wished I had hugged that damn goose. He was, and always will be, The King of the United States.

CHAPTER EIGHT

Bill Kurtis

I have performed for nearly every type of scenario in my 30+ years as an entertainer. I have been a costumed character at amusement parks, a birthday party clown, a Las Vegas headliner, an opening act, a stage and screen actor, and I have danced the Macarena while wearing a chicken suit. I think it's safe to say I am willing to do many things if there's a paycheck involved.

I suppose one could say that my lack of focus on any one particular endeavor has led to my oft-mentioned non-famous status. The argument could be made that, had I focused only on being a comedian for example, I could be doing as well as some of my friends: Kyle Kinane, Pete Holmes, Kumail Nanjiani, Craig Robinson, and T.J. Miller are stellar examples. However, it's difficult to say just who is going to hit and who isn't, and I have always been focused on staying working as opposed to the exact type of work. As long as I was getting a paycheck from the entertainment industry, I was happy to be working.

When I received a call from actor and casting director, Jim Boinski, in September of 2004 checking my availability to work as a *featured extra* on a television program, I was hesitant to take the gig. A featured extra is generally a background player who has no lines, but has specific tasks to perform to further the plot. As an example: for this shoot, they wanted me to play a Capone-era gangster who paid off the police and got beaten in an alley. A regular extra would simply be in the background of a scene, like a restaurant guest or a man in a crowded airport. Featured extras got paid a little more than your standard background player, but it still wasn't a lot of money.

While I have done a fair amount of extra work, not being a union member with SAG or AFTRA meant I wasn't going to get much more than a credit for my resume and some donuts. I knew that the money was probably crap, the hours would probably be long and as boring as possible, but the casting director was a friend of mine and I had nothing going on that day, so I took the job. I'm a lazy person, but I'm also a professional entertainer who values a paycheck. Moreover, pretending that I was going to clean my apartment and get housework or marketing done while knowing I was going to waste the day with cigars, television, and internet porn made taking a paltry paycheck a better plan. Besides, a featured extra had a much better chance at getting some face time on television, and the special we were shooting was guaranteed a slot on the History Channel. I was looking forward to this long day of acting like a mobster because many of my friends were also working the shoot. In fact, I'd been a gangster with this mob countless times before.

If you take work as a theme strolling character in the city of Chicago, you can *always* make a good living as a gangster. It seemed, at least at the time, every company coming to Chicago for a convention wanted a Speakeasy themed event with mobsters and flappers scattered throughout the crowd. You know, a *true* Chicago experience. Get yourself a pinstripe suit, a hat, and a fake Tommy gun, and you can make $100 an hour walking around corporate events in the Chicago area, which is considerably better than the $100 per day I would be making for this TV shoot. OK, I'll stop complaining about the cash.

This gig was being produced, filmed, and edited by Kurtis Productions, which was headed up by legendary golden-throated newsman – and Chicago celebrity – Bill Kurtis. Until cable television took over, Kurtis was only known to Chicagoans. When The History Channel and A&E's Biography series came around, Kurtis became more of a household name. His immediately recognizable voice has narrated more of your favorite programs than you may realize. These days, he is most widely known as the narrator for the *Anchorman* films. I was eager to meet him because he was such a presence in the Chicago media scene. He was also reported to be a hell of a fun guy to work with. I figured the best place to work on my Bill Kurtis impression would be a day of working with him on set.

Kurtis was a very hands-on guy with his productions. I was shocked to see him working the camera, giving direction, moving sets, and doing a lot more grunt work than someone of his status usually would. Certainly someone with his name on the production company didn't usually do this picayune work. Of course, when asked about it, he would say, "Andy, when you are trying to make Mount Olympus, but only have the budget for a sand castle, you grab a shovel yourself." I liked him immediately.

The program we were working on was called *Investigating History: Taking out Al Capone* and it was slated to air on The History Channel on October 25, 2004. The show detailed the little-known story of how six men, none of whom were traditional law enforcement types, were the real masterminds behind the process that lead to the IRS bringing Al Capone to justice. I fully admit, I learned a lot while participating in this program. We shot in late September, so there was a lot of work to be done in a short time. I confess, this was possibly the most fun I've ever had on set. The sheer fact that there was so little turnaround time between shooting and the air date meant we would not have to suffer through the typical "hurry up and wait" aspects of a normal shoot. The scenes were well thought out, planned far in advance, and Kurtis knew exactly what he wanted from his broken-nosed gangsters.

None of us had any lines, so there was never any pressure to mind our words, remember dialogue, or worry about starting and stopping. Our scenes would be intercut among interviews with experts who would chronicle the events which led to the eventual capture and prosecution of Al Capone, but that didn't mean our scenes weren't fun. Our role was to be as outrageous as Capone himself, adding that gangster flair to what would otherwise be a mundane tale of tax evasion. The first scene we shot was in an old Chicago bar which had actually been a speakeasy in Capone's day. Sadly, I forget the name of the bar, but I remember wishing I had known about it years earlier. It was magnificent. A classic looking bar, and the perfect location for this scene.

As gangsters, we were supposed to be living the life: enjoying illegal booze, scoring with sexy flappers, and avoiding the cops. They wanted lots of party atmosphere, smoke, and drinking. We had been asked ahead of time if we were interested in smoking cigars in the scene. Being a big cigar-smoker, I emphatically replied in the affirmative. Kurtis himself handed me a very nice Dominican cigar that cost far too much for the meager budget of this shoot. I lit up, and waited for further direction. My job was easy: drink, flirt with a flapper, and smoke a cigar. The cigar had already been provided, and the flapper turned out to be Kurtis' embarrassed assistant – a very attractive brunette named Joanna. As for the drinks, Kurtis hadn't felt like paying the bar for the use of their bottles, nor did he feel that going the Hollywood route of substituting apple juice for whiskey would be right. "Try this, everyone," Kurtis said. "It's a lovely elderberry wine my wife and I bottled ourselves on our ranch." I asked him why he was serving actual alcohol for this shoot. He simply smiled and said, "Well, Andy, I wanted to feature a real homemade product in mismatched bottles in the scene. I have many bottles of this lovely elderberry wine at the house, so it made sense to me." I looked at him knowing there was more to the story. "Besides, Andy, you know what you are getting paid for this. Take all the perks you can get!" I don't believe I have ever tasted such delicious wine in my life. Best 9 to 11 A.M. wine in the world as far as I can say. I believe this was the second time in my life I got paid to get drunk on the job. The first was several years earlier while filming some industrial film for college students. Ironically, a film about the dangers of collegiate drinking. That time it had been cheap beer. This time it was fresh elderberry wine, and the bartender's pouring hand was *heavy*. Bill really liked sharing his wine with his cast.

What made this scene even better was watching Kurtis behind the camera. Since I had been given his personal assistant to flirt with, he reveled in embarrassing her to the fullest extent. "Woo her, Andy! She is there for you. She is your possession. You will charm her, take her, and cast her aside when you are done." It's as if he was reading my mind. We did our best not to break into hysterics listening to his classic voice directing us in seduction. "That's right, Joanna. Stroke his face a little bit. You want him. Andy is a very powerful man! Touch foreheads. Intimacy is key." She whispered in my ear, "I am so going to kill him at the Christmas party this year!"

Once Kurtis was convinced he had embarrassed Joanna enough, and that he had enough footage of happily drinking gangsters, it was time to move on to the next scene. The rest of the day had us in alleyways running from cops, drinking at bars, and speeding down roads in vintage automobiles. I ended up featured rather prominently in two scenes.

A couple of our gangsters switched costumes and became Chicago policemen who accepted bribery cash from me . . . which I was all too happy to offer them. While setting up the scene, Kurtis kept taking my fedora. Walking around in it, he barked orders with a mobster swagger but the voice of Bill Kurtis. Another outdoor scene featured Capone himself, and Bill kept asking me questions about the era. "Can you imagine a man like him being so brazen as to wear such a brightly colored hat?" Bill was having a blast.

After a few more establishing shots, it was time for a late lunch/early dinner. Getting to eat at any gig was a thrill, but Bill made certain we had a delicious meal at a wonderful place. Of course, there was method to his madness. Being a budget conscious Chicago celebrity, he had been able to secure a great restaurant with that old-school charm. Not wanting to miss an opportunity to film, he had the cameras roll and told us we were shooting a banquet where Capone bludgeoned two mobsters with a baseball bat. "We will get to the murders later. For now, enjoy this sumptuous meal and don't mind us if we film you." He even made certain I had another cigar to enjoy. Before long, we were well fed and ready to watch the blood fly. I was smoking a cigar and we choreographed the action on the spot. I had more than decided this was the most fun I had had in a very long time. Having had a day full of blood, booze, babes, and cigars, I really didn't give a damn about the cash any more.

Once our meal had been eaten, and two gangsters had been thoroughly beaten to death, I was asked if I wouldn't mind getting a little blood on me for the next scene. Wearing a suit I had paid almost three dollars for, I had no reservations about getting a little dirty. I headed to the loading dock of a local meat packing plant where I was informed that I was going to get the ever-living crap beaten out of me by a couple of rival mobsters. My "dead" body would then be dragged through a meat locker. I was thrilled about this. Not only did I know blood would get me on screen, but I would also be able to put a little of my Ringling Bros. slaps and falls training to use. I ended up creating a fight scene with the two other actors and giving Kurtis a few simple ways to capture the action without giving away the fact that I was not being hit at all. We shot the fight from a handful of angles and by the end of the scene, I was a beaten mess with my mouth full of blood and my suit absolutely ruined. From there, I went into corpse mode and we shot a few sequences of me being *dealt with* by a competing gang. What a hoot!

The program aired, and it had turned out beautifully. I ended up with a lot more face time than I expected, and I made certain everyone knew to tune in to the show. Oddly enough, my mother watched and somehow missed seeing me entirely. She didn't recognize the beaten man in the alley, the guy bribing the cop, the man flirting rather professionally with the pretty flapper, or the cigar-smoking man at the banquet. She assumed the fancy shoes being dragged through a meat locker were mine, but she failed to see her son on screen. Interestingly, she did have one question. "What was it like to work with Bill Kurtis?" She had admired him for many years, watching him deliver the news night after night. I told her that Bill, along with everyone under his employ, was an absolute dream to work with. The man makes a mean wine, hires beautiful women as his assistants (Call me, Joanna!), knows the best hidden restaurants in Chicago, and goes out of his way to make you feel special. I'd relive that day again for free if I had the chance.

CHAPTER NINE

Al Jorgensen and C.F. Turner

O ccasionally, I have bumped into famous people when I was off duty. Not all of these encounters provide a tale worth writing about, but an argument *could* be made that this entire book is a collection of stories not worth writing about. While I'm not inclined to disagree with you, I will be quick to tell you "Too late!" I wrote it, you bought it, and I'm grateful.

Al Jorgensen was lead singer for the industrial metal band, Ministry. Outside of that, I know nothing about him except that he was frequently seen in and around

Chicago drinking, seeing other musicians, and being obnoxious. In fact, he was doing those things one particular night when I was seen around Chicago drinking, seeing a musician, and being obnoxious.

It was a Monday night in Chicago. For many years of my life, a Monday night in Chicago meant heading into the city to a great rock dive bar called Lounge Ax. My friend, and very talented musician – Pat McCurdy – had a long-standing regular gig there. I loved having some place fun to go on a Monday night, and it didn't matter if I had to work the next day or not. Mondays meant Lounge Ax, beer, flirting with inaccessible (and oddly attractive) bar staffers, seeing friends, and singing along with Pat.

Oddly enough, the day I, quite literally, bumped into Jourgensen at Lounge Ax, I was talking to my brother and a few other people about him. I still can't name a single Ministry song, but his name would come up in conversations when talking about the many cool venues and shows people had seen in the city. It seemed fans of Ministry and his other band, The Revolting Cocks, had always known of Jourgensen's reputation for rowdy behavior and intoxicated language. Other than what I had heard from my brother and a few friends, I didn't know anything about him until one particular Monday when I arrived at Lounge Ax to see Pat.

Lounge Ax was not a pretty place. It was structurally unsound, and was likely being held together by the endless layers of band bumper stickers and posters. Every toilet had a resident population of fruit flies, the place never smelled of anything one would call pleasant, and there was enough nicotine on the walls to give the paint job cancer. I often wondered how many of the people, especially the women I would see in there every Monday night, would have ever bothered to visit the place if there wasn't a favorite musical act playing. Many a lady has told me about the tremendous amount of forearm strength necessary to hold yourself up on the bars in the bathroom stalls to prevent your most delicate of parts from touching the cracked porcelain toilets. However, the beer selection was decent enough, and everyone was friendly. I saw many great shows there over the years. With all its flaws, Lounge Ax was awesome! Everybody should experience the beauty and majesty of a great rock and roll craphole bar in their lifetime. These are the places where you'll find stellar musical acts, have your best of times, and where you're very likely to get herpes and not be angry about it. Unfortunately, places like this are few and far between in the age of John Taffer and his rescued bars. Lounge Ax attracted all kinds of people, and on any given night *everyone* was welcome . . .

including the front man for an industrial metal band who liked to drink too much.

Apparently, Lounge Ax was a regular hangout for Jourgensen, Pat just wasn't on his list of must-see acts. He had been drinking there prior to my arrival, and I confess I had a few cocktails over dinner with friends beforehand. As I reached to open the door, my hand was nearly broken when Jourgensen tumbled out of the bar, head first, causing the door to fling open rapidly. He nearly shot me to the ground when he fell into me, but I managed to keep my footing, catch the very drunk rock star, and help him right his stance. Of course, I was not exactly nice about the process.

"Hey! Watch it, *asshole*!" I was a little buzzed, so yeah that was the cleverest phrase this author could come up with. Sorry. He shrugged his shoulders, and in the gruff voice of who'd had many too many said, "Fuck you! Do you have *any* idea who I am?" Now, I may have been a little intoxicated, but I was definitely not so far gone that I couldn't think of something clever to say in reply. I looked at him up and down, and an expression of total recognition and regret washed over my face. "Oh! Oh my God. I am so sorry." I brushed off the sleeve of his arm with deference. He stood a little straighter and waited for me to apologize further. "My fault. I *do* know who you are. You are an *ASSHOLE*!" I walked into the bar.

My friend, a big Ministry fan, said, "Dude! You just called Al Jourgensen an asshole. That's fantastic!"

I know. That's a long way to go to get to, "You're an asshole." Sue me! You can donate this book to a library later. For now, let's flip to the other side of the record as I tell you about the time I met the bass player for Bachman Turner Overdrive, C.F. Turner, at a Fourth of July festival.

While living in the Chicago suburb, Hoffman Estates, I was somewhat out of the entertainment business and spending time in a more pedestrian setting with a "real job". Miraculously, I didn't have to work the weekend of July 4th, and our local park was having a festival. I was a little melancholy at the time because I was not out of the business by choice; the girl I was dating at the time had forced the mini retirement on me. On any other July 4th, I would have been working. That being said, my mood brightened when I realized I would get to watch fireworks for the first time in many years, and that the headlining act for this particular event was Canadian classic rock group, Bachman Turner Overdrive.

I was very much surprised to see them at this event; it definitely wasn't the largest of the many city festivals throughout the Chicagoland area that day. I was even

happier when I found out it was a free show. Spend the
night drinking a few beers and listening to some rock
tunes instead of selling video games at the local toy
store? Sign me the hell *up*!

After checking out some of the rides and games, and
consuming a few adult beverages, my then-girlfriend
and I decided to find a place in front of the stage where
we could see the band. The fest was pretty empty, but
we decided it would be best to stake our claim to a good
spot early on and maintain our real estate by alternating
food and drinks duty for an hour or so.

During one of my beverage trips, which should have
been the last one before the band took the stage, I noticed a man who looked decidedly more weathered than
most in this particular suburb. Were my older siblings
not ten years older than me, I might not have been as
familiar with the music of BTO, and I wouldn't have recognized C. F. Turner. I didn't have the best view, but I
was pretty certain he was in front of me at the beer tent.

Turner is a gravelly-looking man; I've always
thought he looked like every biker on every Harley t-
shirt ever made. I didn't know much about him personally since I was just an appreciator of their music and not
an invested fan, but I definitely recognized him when he

turned from the beer line with an armload of Budweiser and slammed right into me.

He immediately apologized for bumping into me, and asked if I was all right. Perhaps he was so polite because he knew he was at fault, but I'm pretty certain it was because he's Canadian. They are arguably the most polite people in the universe. Seriously, Canadians will apologize for a sunny day if given the chance. I assured him there was no harm done, and asked, "Aren't you C. F. Turner?" He replied, "Yeah. That's why I was in such a hurry. We have to get started soon." Confused, I looked at the many bottles of Bud in his arms. I asked, "Did you run out of beer in the trailer?" He laughed. "Nah, all they have is that Heineken shit in there. Not our speed." We both laughed, and I told him to drink up and have a good show. "My girlfriend and I will be ready." At that, he handed me two cold beers and said, "Enjoy." Apologizing one last time for bumping into me, he left. As the first chords began, my girlfriend and I clinked our bottles and drank a toast to the band.

I learned a lot from these encounters. Both of these guys were legitimate rock stars. Both were in a public setting, and had drink on their minds. One managed to be cordial while the other was nothing but angry. I've tried to imagine how I would act were I ever to achieve any level of notoriety. I like to think that I would be more of the beer-giving, apologetic, polite kind rather than the bitter drunk, but I admit, I've been both. What I have not been is famous. Perhaps one day, I'll be that, too.

CHAPTER TEN

Sam Phillips

The first time I was booked to perform at the Market Street Festival in Columbus, Mississippi, I think I was more excited about traveling through Memphis than I was the rather good paycheck I'd be receiving. At the time, Memphis was one of the many places I'd always wanted to visit, but hadn't yet found the time, or the resources, to make it happen. Being spring, there weren't a lot of bookings in the Chicago area; there isn't a lot of work in May or November. This meant that I not only had a good chunk of change waiting for me in Mississippi, but I had a little bit of freedom to pad my trip with an extra day of fun. I was Memphis bound.

Knowing that I hoped to visit Memphis with my then-wife one day, I chose not to do *everything* on my visiting wish list. Being an Elvis fan as well as a fan of cheesy tourist traps, however, I simply had to visit Graceland. If you haven't been there, I can't recommend it highly enough. Yes, it's a bit tacky, and yes, watching the hardcore Elvis fans openly sobbing at the grave site is a bit off-putting. That being said, Graceland is worth every penny you'll spend. It's American success meeting American excess that accepts American Express. If you're even remotely a fan of Elvis or rock music, it's a must-see. Of course, the bigger attraction for this music-lover was the Sun Records studio.

Johnny Cash, Jerry Lee Lewis, Carl Perkins, Roy Orbison, the aforementioned Elvis Presley, and countless others have recorded some of the world's most memorable and certainly, game-changing music. After a full tour of the Presley estate, I couldn't wait to get over to Sun.

If they haven't done it yet, I truly believe Memphis would do itself a huge favor by organizing an entire day of historic recording studio tours or one-time homes of legendary performers. Sun Records, if not all of Memphis, is holy ground in my book. Not the book you're reading now, my proverbial *Life Book*

The tour of Sun Studios was inexpensive, and the tiny building oozed energy and history. I know it sounds corny, but some places just have a vibe about them. Had I ever visited the Sun building during the days when it was a butcher shop or a hair salon, even if I had not known it was once a recording studio, I would have been able to feel something powerful about the place. Some locations command that kind of respect from its visitors, and I was excited before I even started the tour.

There are only a few times in my life when I have truly *geeked out* over something or someone. This was one of those times. I listened to the well-rehearsed tour speech coming from the friendly tour guide. I looked at all of the original records on the wall. I posed for a photo with a microphone Elvis supposedly used. I was in love with the place from minute one. I ended up staying in the recording studio a good half hour longer than the rest of the group so I could get more photos and simply soak in the history. I dreamt about what songs may have been recorded in each section of the room and hoped to hear whispers from the greats. After the tour, I spent a long time in the studio store buying some CDs (get the complete recordings of The Prisonaires, by the way).

On my way out, I noticed two gentlemen walking towards this shrine to rock music. They were chatting rather hurriedly, almost with anticipation, At least, that's how I hoped they were talking. I wanted them to be fanboy-geeks like me, eager to hear the stories about the birth of rock n' roll. One man was doing most of the talking. He had on a black satin jacket, dark blue jeans, and boots. His eyes were covered by a pair of amber sunglasses, and he had longer hair and a thick moustache and beard. He was pointing at the sign, the building, and the surroundings, while his friend nodded and listened intently. I was snapping a few photos of the outside of the building when the pair stopped next to me. I took it upon myself to add to their conversation; to speak as one of the newly enlightened who had just finished a musical holy pilgrimage. "It's kind of overwhelming, isn't it?" I said. The bearded man looked at me, and in a cocky, dismissive tone said, "I've seen it, kid!" I just laughed and nodded as if to say, "OK, then. Enjoy!"

As I made my way to my car, I replayed the many wonderful experiences in my head, particularly that last exchange. I had been taken aback by the quip from the stranger, but he seemed familiar to me somehow. Then it hit me like a piano falling from the sky in a classic Tex Avery cartoon. I turned around and really looked at the guy. As he kept talking and pointing, I noticed the Sun Records logo on the back of his jacket. The man who'd "seen it" was the man who'd created it, Sam Phillips. Just like in a movie, the second I realized who he was, he shot a glance back in my direction, nodded, and opened the door to his legacy.

I wanted to go back and shake his hand or try to get a photo with him, but realized I already looked like the biggest, and possibly *worst*, music nerd of all time. I laughed at myself. It wasn't like I didn't know what the guy looked like; Lord knows I had seen several interviews with the guy, not to mention all of the photos I had just seen *everywhere* during today's tour. I simply couldn't go back in there and do anything to redeem myself. Besides, this particular brush with fame couldn't have been any more perfect.

CHAPTER ELEVEN

Isaac Hayes and Donald "Duck" Dunn

One year after I didn't recognize Sam Phillips in Memphis, I found myself booked at the Market Street Festival once again. You've gotta love repeat bookings! This time, I made certain to have even more time off so I could turn it into a bit of a working vacation and bring my then-wife, April, along. The plan was to not only enjoy Memphis, but check out a concert

in nearby Tupelo, soak in some real southern hospitality
(and *food*) in Mississippi and Tennessee, see the Memphis Zoo, head back to Graceland, and see if the Stax
Museum had reached its completion.

The Stax record label — as well as their other label,
Volt — released some of my all-time favorite songs.
While I've always enjoyed Motown music, in my personal
opinion, most of those songs simply can't hold a candle
to the Stax records. Where Motown was very polished
and elegant, Stax and Volt brought an amazing rough
quality to soul, R&B, and rock music. Plus, in their early
days, there was a lot of integration among the bands.
Black and white artists came together to simply make
great music, creating a distinctive sound, a wicked back
beat, and damn near the most memorable hooks in music
history. Booker T. and the M.G.'s, Otis Redding, Sam
and Dave, Rufus Thomas, and countless others changed
music forever in the hallowed halls of the Stax studio.

We didn't have smart phones at the time, and could
only find so much information about the place online before making our journey. Eventually, we found a long-
time local who knew exactly where it was and gave us
directions in his garbled, rustic, southern voice. Miraculously, his directions were spot on.

Even though the building looked exactly like all of the photos I had ever seen of the Stax studio, the museum had a very *new* quality to it. As it happened, it looked new because every bit of it had been accurately recreated from scratch as the original building had been demolished some years earlier. There simply hadn't been a building to put a museum in. This upset me a little bit because I had been looking forward to being in *the* building, but the fact that it was able to rise from the ashes at all was nothing less than a miracle to the locals.

April and I arrived eager to see everything. We walked inside and saw a few reporters from local newspapers and television stations. I assumed it was for the *Memphis Comes Home* concert I had heard about, which was set to feature many Memphis music legends; specifically, Stax/Volt artists. We were both surprised to find out the museum we were standing in was not technically open; we had walked in on press day for the Museum's grand opening weekend. On-hand were museum donors, V.I.P.'s, and invited guests, and we ended up mingling with them all in the gift shop. After giving us a cool booklet and other info about museum membership and their grand opening, the museum director mentioned to us that they were giving the first trial run of the tours and exhibits a few hours later. She welcomed the chance to hear feedback from someone with no personal connection to the place, and offered a friendly invitation to come back. An opportunity to take the first tour ever given at a brand new museum, before the place is officially open to the public? *Yes, please!* But first, we were in a brand new museum, and that meant a gift shop to explore.

As expected, there was a wide array of t-shirts, shot glasses, and music-centric memorabilia. We watched as many a reporter came in and out, and many a cameraman captured *B-roll* footage for news broadcasts. April and I were already buzzing about the prospect of taking the unofficial first tour of the place when I suddenly saw her face freeze with happy excitement. I asked her what was up, and she motioned for me to turn around. As I did, I heard one of the most distinctive and recognizable voices ever heard. The voice was what had first caught my wife's attention, and the voice told me we were about to enjoy something very special.

"Is that Isaac Hayes?" I asked the museum director. With a huge smile, she motioned with her index finger to remain quiet and whispered, "Yes!" I admit, I was a little disappointed when she didn't say, "Yer damn right!"

We asked if it would be ok to introduce ourselves to him, and she said, "As soon as he is done with his interview, go right ahead. He's *great!*" I looked over at April and mumbled under my breath, "This day just got awesome!" Softly, she replied, "Um . . . *yeah!*"

We patiently waited for him to finish his interview and make the day for a few very flustered female fans. Hayes was gracious and personable, and he had time for everyone who wanted to meet with him. When it was our turn to meet the legend, I had no idea the man belonging to the voice was not a ten-foot tall superhero covered in a fuzzy shag vest with no shirt, and skin-tight pants in animal print. Rather, he was a thin man a tad shorter than I was. Nonetheless, he was Isaac freakin' Hayes, and he was eager to meet with us.

He immediately gravitated to my lovely wife, and I expected nothing less. He was a most outgoing and flirtatious man, but never disrespectful to either of us. He was very interested in what brought us to the museum and our lives in general. I had recently worked a series of gigs at one of his BBQ joints near Chicago, and he had some great stories about the good times he'd had in our neck of the woods. While we did not get a photo with him, we asked if he would sign our souvenir program from the museum. He personalized it, asking our names once again. Realizing my wife's name was April, he took her hand and began to serenade her right there in the gift shop. He belted out a few lines from the Pat Boone hit "April Love" in his deep voice, bringing a big smile to her face, and a loud set of school-girl screams from the other female Hayes' fans still in the room. I don't think there was a fully breathing woman in the room after that.

As Mr. Hayes made his exit, we were buzzing with excitement. The museum operator had really taken a liking to us, and was overjoyed that we'd gotten that moment. I think knowing we had come just to see the museum without knowing if the place was even open or not told her beyond any shadow of a doubt that we were *fans* of the great music Stax produced. She reminded us when the first preview tour was scheduled to begin, and suggested some nearby places to eat and things to do. "You're not far from Graceland. You can have lunch, see Graceland, and be back in plenty of time." Being people who can take a hint, we went for lunch and to visit The King.

This being my second time at Graceland, I was very happy to be able to show it to April. It really was the sort of tacky fun we always loved to visit. So many wonderful exhibits, and even better people-watching, was there for our amusement. While at the hallowed ground for all

Elvis fans, we learned a few very important things. First of all, nobody, and I mean *nobody,* at Graceland, whether they are employees or fans, can fathom touring the complex without getting the pre-recorded headset tour accessory. The very thought of us looking, reading the signs, and asking questions of the docents simply made heads spin. Next, apparently there is no such thing as "too much shag" or "too gaudy" when it comes to accoutrements in The King's castle. Lastly, and I cannot stress this enough, when you are standing in front of Elvis' grave site, fight every urge you may have to reenact the "too much fucking perspective" scene from *This is Spinal Tap.* I promise you, the likelihood of there being anyone there who thinks it's as funny as you do is very slim.

As much fun as Graceland was, and as delicious as our meal was, we couldn't wait to get back to Stax. Every few minutes, wherever we were, one of us would look at the other with a "that was so freaking cool". Many times, one of us would lean towards the other one and say, "*Isaac Hayes!*" The day was already perfect in our minds, but we still wanted to be among the first to take that tour!

Upon reentering the building, the museum operator was delighted to see us. She put the guest book in front of us and we were happy to sign it. Not being officially open to the public meant they couldn't charge the full amount for the tour. We asked what that charge would be, and then donated that amount to the museum, which made the director very happy. Inside we went.

The museum was simply a tribute to music and a haven for music-lovers of all ages. Each exhibit was well thought out and professionally executed. There were many interactive sections and countless rooms full of historical artifacts. It seemed less like we were in a museum and more like we were a part of a city-wide celebration. It was everything we were hoping for and more.

Not even halfway through the tour, our now good friend from the museum found us. We both thought she was checking in to see if there was as much impact from the exhibits as she'd hoped. Rather, she whispered in my ear, "Would you like to meet Duck Dunn?"

If you are unfamiliar with the late, great Donald "Duck" Dunn and his remarkably huge impact on modern rock, R&B, and soul music, we can cease being friends right now. By all means, finish this book, but do not expect me to look your way if we cross paths.

Duck Dunn was arguably the *best* bass player in the world. If not the best, certainly one of the most recorded and most influential. He and his partner, Steve Cropper, were probably on more hit records than any two people on the planet. Just watch *The Blues Brothers* and you'll know who I'm talking about.

As a kid, I was practically raised on *The Blues Brothers* movie, and I listened to the soundtrack almost daily. From there, I started digging deeper and finding where all this incredible music had come from. Eventually, I had the first CD boxset featuring all of the Stax singles from their earliest days. Were it possible to wear down a CD the way you could a record, I'm certain I would have scrubbed all nine of those CDs clean. The thought of meeting Mr. Dunn was mind-blowing. Asking me if I wanted to meet him was a little like asking a ten-year-old boy from my generation if he wanted to meet Hank Aaron or Pete Rose. I couldn't say "*Yes!*" fast enough.

She told me that he'd just entered the tour area, and pointed me in his general direction. Once I'd found him, he was all too happy to speak with me and give me some real time to be a complete music geek with him. My wife found a scrap of paper and a pen for me to grab an autograph, and he very graciously signed it, asking me about my life and how I came to find the museum. Truthfully, I just wanted to thank him for being on so many of my favorite songs. I could barely contain myself while talking to him.

It wasn't long before he humbly asked if our time could come to an end. He explained with a tear in his eye that the location of the museum had been lost, and had been reborn. We were standing in the recreated studio, on the exact spot where so many of his groundbreaking performances were recorded. Trying to hold back tears, he said, "This is truly an emotional experience for me and I want to soak it all in. I apologize if I am being rude."

It was at that moment I noticed we were not just in the spot where some of the world's greatest hits were recorded, but we were in front of Dunn's favorite bass guitar. Nearly everything he'd recorded, nearly every tour, and nearly every note that had made his career so extraordinary had been played on that very bass. I have been privy to many surreal moments in my life, but watching Donald Dunn look at his own guitar in a museum may top the list. A museum piece being witnessed by the person who made it museum-worthy in the very room where the history happened will stay with me for the rest of my life.

After we finished our tour — concluded by an intimidating and massive wall of singles, albums, and CDs put out by Stax and Volt — we couldn't wait to thank the museum director for all the wonderful memories. She was as big a fan as we were, and she actually *apologized* for not being able to introduce us to Mavis Staples and Steve Cropper, who had been there briefly. We laughed and told her we'd forgive her.

Assuming it's still on display, you can still find our names in the guest book at the Stax Museum. My now ex-wife proudly displays the program featuring Isaac Hayes's signature, and on my wall you will find a small, framed scrap of yellow legal paper with the signature of Donald "Duck" Dunn. They've both passed since our incredible day with them. Would I go back to the Stax Museum of Soul Music again? Yer damn right!

CHAPTER TWELVE

Koko Taylor and Buddy Guy

K oko Taylor was a powerful voice in blues music, and unquestionably beloved in and around Chicago. You can listen to any of her recordings and be blown away by her sheer presence as a vocalist. Having been a blues fan for more years than I can remember, I can say with certainty that she has more than earned her spot on the mountaintop as one of the all-time greats. She was also the last person I expected to meet at a showcase of new homes in southwest suburban Plainfield, Illinois.

I had worked a few of these events in the past, and they were, for the most part, boring as hell. Basically, some real estate development company gets a handful of contractors to build spec houses in a soon-to-be-perfectly carved out portion of former Illinois farmland. If you've ever seen a piece of suburban landscape where all the houses look the same except for one block, that's where the neighborhood was initially developed.

There were about ten or twenty different styles of homes on display from several contractors, and realtors on hand to get you in on the ground floor of development. My job, as a juggling clown, was to keep the children of yuppie families entertained while mommy and daddy looked at houses and decided whether or not they could afford to build a house from scratch. What was worse, there wasn't a spec playground for the kids, so I had to wander from house to house hoping to find families with kids to distract so some contractor could explain why their Ranch style home was better than the one down the street. You know, because random clowns walking around neighborhoods looking for kids isn't weird or anything. This was a long weekend for me, and really dreadful as far as gigs went. I was fortunate enough to find a few other entertainer friends to talk to during down time, and I managed to make the hours pass by, one balloon animal or juggling maneuver at a time.

I got to know this particular fake neighborhood very well, and made regular rounds of every house. I can't lie. I got to a point where I stopped most often at the houses with the best refreshments. Houses are more appealing with fresh baked cookies, even if you have no intention of buying one. If I couldn't find people to entertain, at least I was going to eat well. After leaving a house with the most delicious miniature brunch pastries, I detoured from my rounds to head back toward a house I had visited only a few minutes ago. Why the detour? I simply couldn't believe I was hearing Koko Taylor singing in this spec neighborhood, and I had to see for myself.

Sure enough, I made my way through the decent-sized crowd of people, and there was the blues legend herself singing an acapella version of her signature tune *Wang Dang Doodle* for a local news crew. It seems this particular contractor felt baked goods and sandwiches weren't what this part of town wanted, so they brought in the big voice of Koko Taylor.

This was one of those times in my life when I wished I wasn't clad in clown attire for an event. I have no idea why it made a difference to me, but the thought of meeting musical royalty like her while reeking of clown white and baby powder turned my stomach. In my mind, Koko was to be treated with reverence, not to be greeted by a circus clown. That didn't seem to matter to her, however; she was all too eager to say hi to this colorful young man rambling off album titles and songs from her past as I completely geeked out. I'm certain you could see a flushed, and somewhat embarrassed, face through all that makeup as I told her something ridiculous like, "You sing right *through* me, Miss Taylor. These walls aren't strong enough for your voice." She was as delightful as I had always heard she was; gracious, bubbly, energetic, and captivating. If I hadn't known who she was, I would have thought she was one of the sweet ladies who baked cookies for these houses.

After a few moments of fanboy worship, she had to make her way back to the news crew and exit the building. My one lasting memory of Taylor, aside from her voice and her generosity with her time, was her big laugh when she said to me, "I do believe this is the first time in my life when I heard a clown say the phrase, 'Wang Dang Doodle.'" In a long and storied career like hers, I suppose I owe a debt of gratitude to Ringling Bros. for being able to represent a first for her. I was even more grateful I hadn't been booked as a mime.

Love or hate the fact that I frequently met someone I idolized dressed as someone, or something else entirely, there are certainly times that I wouldn't have met them at all were it not for my choice of career and costume. Were it not for realtors needing a clown to eat their cookies, I wouldn't have met Koko Taylor. Had a corporate event not needed a singing Blues Brothers act, I wouldn't have worked with another of the biggest names in blues, Buddy Guy

Buddy Guy is one of the greats; masterful guitar player, bold vocalist, charismatic performer, and fun personality all rolled into one. I have always enjoyed his rougher approach to softer songs, and he has definitely earned his stripes in blues music. Hell, he's earned the whole damned zebra.

Much like the story about Audrey Hepburn, I didn't get to shake hands with this revered guitar player, and I didn't get an autograph, photograph or even a guitar pick from him. I did get to work with him which would have been enough, but even better, I got paid to hear him play. Not a bad deal at all.

This particular event was held at the Sheraton Grand Chicago —I can't tell you how many times I've worked in that building. All in all, it was a pretty basic Blues Brothers gig for me and my partner, Jim. By this point, Jim and I had probably worked over a hundred shows as the duo, and we were one of the busiest acts in town. For this event, we did a little meet and greet with the party guests during the cocktail hour and dinner. After dinner, we performed a three-song set of Blues Brothers tunes. While there were many folks impersonating the Blues Brothers for corporate events in the Chicago area, many of them did not sing. They might be great for posing for photos, but if you wanted more you came to us or a handful of our competitors.

We were also very reasonably priced. We offered packages with bands of varying size, as well as what's called a track show. A track show is essentially a singer performing to karaoke tracks rather than a band. Surprisingly, there are Blues Brothers acts who sell their whole experience by lip-syncing. The Blues Brothers are popular in the Midwest! A three-song set like this one was like second nature to us by then. Start off with "Gimme Some Lovin'", head into "Soul Man", and finish with "Sweet Home Chicago". Pay the men!

From the day the client contacted us for the event, there was an unusual sense of clandestine secrecy to everything. We were told we would be there to warm up the audience for their headliner, but we weren't allowed to know who the headliner was. I believe this was a celebration show for a wildly successful sales team, and the company showed their appreciation by surprising them with a big-name act. In the beginning, we didn't really care who the headliner was, we just wished they'd tell us so we'd know if we were charging too little cash. Either way, a gig was a gig and we were happy to do it.

In subsequent conversations to confirm details, the client made it even more apparent that she had a secret and she wanted to tell someone who the headliner was, but couldn't; it was a little like being around a six-year-old who had just been told a secret, the temptation to tell someone was that great. She held her ground, but her enthusiasm started to make us wonder. Since I was the one pretending to be someone who could sing, I really wanted to know just so I would be prepared for the level of embarrassment I would feel. I've always felt I have a perfect voice for the blues, but when I'm surrounded by real singers I believe I have a perfect voice for comedy. The weeks went by and the phone calls continued. Still no name.

The day of our appearance finally arrived. There was a stage in the dining area, and adjacent to our banquet hall was a second room partitioned off by a temporary wall. The idea was that we would do our set then lead the people into the next room where there were bars, desserts, and their secret special guest. We were to act as the Pied Pipers of fun for these folks. When we arrived at the Sheraton and met our client, she still didn't want a living soul to know who the headliner was. She wouldn't even tell us for fear that we'd ruin her surprise.

We had played along during all of the phone conversations, but now we *had* to know. We explained to her that she was the only person at her company that we knew. She had obviously kept this secret from everyone, including her boss who had asked *us* if we knew anything about it. I believe I was the one who came up with the story that tipped the scale in our direction and convinced her to give up the ghost. I told her not knowing might affect my performance. Everyone knew they were in for a treat, but we frequently would reference great blues acts in the show. Knowing who was in the other room would guarantee we didn't accidentally blow the show for her by saying his or her name. Mind you, this was total BS, but it got us the name.

We were both impressed to hear it was Buddy Guy. We had narrowed the list down to a few names, and he'd made our short list. We were also pleased we hadn't known ahead of time. I mean, we really were a great Blues Brothers act, but that had more to do with how much fun we had on stage and less to do with our singing ability. Naturally, I was pleased to be spared several weeks panicking about pretending to sing the blues in front of a guy who had practically invented them. Good news: I was going to open for Buddy Guy. Bad news: By comparison, I sucked!

After some discussion as to whether or not we should change our game plan, we decided to be the act they hired. After all, they loved our video and CD, we had done plenty of these shows before, and we were damn good. Moreover, it's the blues. We can be bad as long as people feel good. We did our set and received fantastic applause and laughter from the crowd. As we were singing, I kept noticing a partition in the wall next to the stage opening up, and a head peering out to watch. Every time it opened, I tried to catch a glimpse of who was checking us out. Every time, it was Buddy Guy watching us perform rather hackneyed but enjoyable versions of classic tunes. From what I could gather, he seemed to be enjoying our performance and nodding in approval which made me happy. At one point, he caught my attention and gave me a big smile and a thumbs up.

The last notes of "Sweet Home Chicago" started to play, the applause died down, and we began leading everyone over to the next room when Buddy Guy jumped in and continued to play "Sweet Home Chicago" in the same key. The music never stopped, and we told everyone to follow the blues to the next room. When we had almost everyone in the adjacent room, Buddy began to sing. No intro, no bravado, just the polka-dotted appearance and machine gun guitar playing the blues legend had come to be known for.

He was very gracious to take some time to thank the Blues Brothers once again for opening up the show and even let out an enthusiastic, "Man, were they good!" He could have been full of crap. He could have meant that the *real* Blues Brothers were good, but I choose to believe he was sincere and that he approved of our program. It makes me feel better about myself so, let me have this! Besides, I had just opened for Buddy Guy. How could I feel any less than great?

I took pride in knowing the audience was very well warmed up, and a lot of folks asked why we weren't singing with Buddy. Some were even disappointed we weren't the main act. I shook my head in amazement at those statements. We explained that they were in the presence of blues royalty, and would soon forget the fake Blues Brothers. I told one woman, "I get to play a blues legend for a little while. He gets to be a blues legend every day. I am certain you'll hear a big difference soon enough." He broke into his rendition of "Mustang Sally" and she ran toward the stage.

CHAPTER THIRTEEN

Tai Babilonia and Randy Gardner

I used to love watching the Olympics. Summer or Winter Games, I didn't care. I remember them being truly wonderful and memorable experiences for me when I was a kid. I got caught up in all the hype, the pageantry, the sportsmanship, and the world politics of it all —Damn you, East German judges! The Olympics were both exciting and frustrating for me. The concept of something happening every four years, like an election or a graduation, was fascinating to me, and seeing the world come together for athletic competition with sports common and uncommon to us American kids was thrilling. However, as a kid raised on television, living in an era with only three major networks and PBS, the thought of something so important it would dominate the entirety of the programming on one of those three networks was infuriating. After a while, no matter what the sport, regardless of your degree of interest, some sports are just too boring to stomach. Seriously, why couldn't the Olympics be more like *ABC's Wide World of Sports*? At least then you could see barrel-jumping. Why the hell is there no barrel-jumping in the Olympics? Bring Back Barrel Jumping! Anyway . . .

These days I don't think anyone other than the competing athletes care about the Olympics; they simply aren't special anymore. Now that the Summer and Winter Olympics have been staggered, we're forced to endure Badminton or the Luge every two years. There isn't really a sense of anticipation or excitement about The Games. They're also known to be among the most corruptly run in all of sports with illegalities in their business model so abhorrent, even the mafia doesn't want a piece of the action. More and more of the amateur athletes are actually professionals, so the thrill of watching the world's upstarts claiming a gold medal just isn't there. I mean, does *anyone* get a thrill out of watching the USA Men's Basketball team destroy nations where a basketball is considered a luxury item? Moreover, there are now thousands of channels available to the viewer, with more entertaining options to cure boredom than any level of phony amateur competition can muster. I'll take my least favorite episode of *American Pickers* over my favorite Olympic sport every time. When there were only a few networks out there, the Olympics were a part of every American's conversation for the entire two weeks of play. Every single bit of sorrow or pain, every moment of glory or grief, and every story of triumph and tragedy was on our collective mind. Now? Who gives a damn? Rarely do we hear about the amazing feats of athleticism or the victory over a hated nation. Now, if we hear anything about the Olympics it has to do with a terrorist bombing, a disease-filled ocean, an unscrupulous organizational committee, a figure skater getting cracked in the knee, or any time a swimmer has been caught smoking pot, banging another athlete, or trashing a bathroom. It simply isn't the same.

Perhaps that's why meeting Olympic Superstars Tai Babilonia and Randy Gardner was quite a thrill for me. They were part of The Games when they were still special, and they were front page news every day. As a ten-year-old boy living in rural Illinois in 1980, I wasn't a big fan of figure skating (I'm still not, really). Still, I was glued to the set every night hoping to watch them dazzle even the most bitter of oppressive judges and take home a gold medal. They were big names in our household and everywhere we went. I was as overjoyed to see them achieve as I was heartbroken when a groin injury dashed their chances at victory. I cannot think of too many times in the modern era of multi-channel television programming when I have cared so much. Although, I do recall loving every second of watching young and injured Kerri Strug take one for the team and land that vault. I was very jaded with regard to The Games by then, but when she stuck that landing and injured herself further to become a hero, she put the limp back in the Olympics. Hey-ohhhh! Try the veal!

I met Olympic Figure Skating's tragic heroes while working as a Blues Brother at a corporate event in a downtown Chicago hotel. If I remember correctly, this was a technical conference for a lot of boffins and tech-heads from the Microsoft Corporation; so basically, it was an extended cocktail party with more drinks, food, and entertainment than most conferences. Interestingly, the client had booked several rooms for different types of fun: one room had adult carnival games, another was set up like a blues lounge, and celebrities were signing autographs in another. Our job was to stroll through the crowds in every room and interact with people.

In the blues lounge, I met a woman named Queenie. She was a wonderful blues singer who had played Koko Taylor in a made-for-television movie. She insisted I come onstage and sing a blues duet with her and her killer band. When they started into a song I had never heard before, I leaned in and quietly told her I didn't know the words. She just smiled and whispered back, "It's the blues, Sugar. Make something up." I was in for an interesting night.

Tai and Randy were in the autograph room stationed at a table with a stack of photos. There wasn't anything advertising their presence or a tie-in to the conference, so they were looking rather bored. In full Blues Brothers attire, and ready for a short break, Jim and I headed over to talk to a couple of sports champions. One of my reasons to chat with them was that my then-wife's grandmother was a *huge* figure skating fan. I simply had to seize the opportunity to get them to sign a photo for her, ensuring my hero status with her.

I think they were as thrilled to see us as we were to meet them. As I said, there weren't a ton of people in their room. There wasn't even a bar in that room to draw guests in. Our presence started to attract a few more people, and I began introducing party guests to "my next ex-wife, Tai Babilonia." If that got a laugh, I'd follow with "You can call her .Tai Baby'." I am fairly certain we were the only entertainment the skaters had the entire evening, and when things quieted down again we

talked about their present-day careers, their championships, and their fateful trip to the 1980 Olympics. They
were a charming couple who offered us a glimpse into
the life of athletes after the championship days, and I
enjoyed meeting them very much.

Since we, dressed as celebrities, were sitting at a table with actual celebrities who were signing photographs, people began to ask if we had photos to sign. Jim
always had promotional materials and other things in his
character briefcase, so he took out a few 8 x 10 photos
and we started signing them. There was just one little
problem. I was clearly *not* the Jake to Jim's Elwood in
the photo. Jim had worked with a different impersonator
named Lou Dellis, and Lou was a spot on lookalike for
John Belushi. When Lou started a family and a different
job, I took over, but we were left with a stack of great
photos which did not feature me as Jake. Our solution to
this any time we signed photos was to deface the image
as much as possible. Like bored adolescents in class, we
would black out teeth, draw on silly moustaches, and
doodle all over the image. Sometimes I would sign the
photo "Not Jake" and draw an arrow to Lou and Jim. It
was a comical solution to a silly problem.

The lovely Babilonia noticed I was scrawling facial
hair all over the Jake, and realized it wasn't me in the
photo. She and Randy both started laughing when they

saw some of the pictures we were handing out to party guests. Before long, she had grabbed one of their glossy photos and started doctoring it up with her pen. Randy grabbed the picture from her and joined in. They were laughing at each other's artwork like kids and really let loose on each other. You could see the good years of being partnered together coming out in a bit of playful disobedience, and the photo they created represented a great bit of behind-the-scenes fun for them. I had to have it.

I got them to sign a photo for April's grandmother with little effort, but I had to *work* to get the other photo from them. They were concerned the image would get out into the world. They had spent a lifetime together building a brand, an identity, and a persona of grace, beauty, and elegance. Even though they were only making occasional appearances on the ice these days, they were very protective of their public image; as if they were always trying to live up to that championship status or constantly trying to live down the day Olympic gold fell through their fingers. That was the reason I wanted the photo for my wall — that rare moment of genuine levity and relaxation they had as just Tai and Randy. Figure skating, much like professional dancing, is dependent upon absolute perfection, impossible standards of grace, and in insane amount of work and dedication. I have always said professional dancers are the only artists who truly love their work, because they make the least amount of money and are never told their performance was good enough. Sure they get applause, but they are trained from an early age that any imperfection ruins the performance, whether the crowd noticed it or not. I have always heard figure skaters suffer the same level of intolerant expectation. To me, that photo was a real moment of joy shared by two people who had been both honored and hurt by the idea of perfection. I could see it on their faces as they doodled on each other's images; it simply had never occurred to them to scribble on a photo and look goofy rather than graceful. This was much better than a signed photo in my opinion.

After a lot of begging, reassuring, and an explanation of *why* I wanted the photo, they conceded and handed me the photo. Tai even wrote "We are so cute!" on it. It hangs on my wall to this .day. I made them a solemn promise I would never share the image online or in print, and I am happy to keep that promise. Rather than share the image, I feel honored that I get to share my memory of them where I will always see them as beautifully human.

CHAPTER FOURTEEN

Michael Jordan

As I've mentioned, I worked in one of the busiest, if not *the* busiest, Blues Brothers impersonation acts in the city of Chicago. I can't lie, putting on the hat, tie, and sunglasses was a fun gig almost every time. In Chicago, there are a few iconic fictional characters that always get a royal treatment. Bozo the Clown, Garfield Goose, Cuddly Duddly, and the Blues Brothers are high on that list. Working as a Blues Brother, whether strolling through a corporate cocktail party or taking the stage with a band, I never felt like my presence wasn't appreciated by all in attendance. That reverence is what made it possible for me to be in the same room, or in this case, the same elevator, with people like Michael Jordan and Doug Collins.

My Elwood partner — Jim Bina of Custom Comedy Capers — and I were booked a Chicago hotel hosting a party for an organization that specialized in the needs of hemophiliac children. The event promised food, fun, and an appearance by the *Bluez* Brothers — we didn't want to get our asses sued. We were slated to take photos with the kids and their families and sing a handful of songs while the children danced and nervous parents prayed none of them fell and scraped a knee.

As luck would have it, this also happened to be a uniquely special night for the city of Chicago. The Washington Wizards basketball team was in town, making this the first time all-star great, Michael Jordan, returned to Chicago to play since leaving the Bulls franchise.

If the aforementioned fictional characters were icons, Al Capone, Harry Caray, the '85 Chicago Bears, and Michael Jordan were *Gods*. To say this was a big story for the area is a massive understatement. Michael Jordan returning to Chicago to play against the team he had won so many championships with was not just a local story, it was international news. I had never seen so many different press organizations from so many different countries at any single event in my life, including the Washington Press Club dinner, massive sporting events, political rallies, and major motion pictures I had the pleasure of working over the years. *Nothing* compared to the level of press in attendance that night the Washington Wizards arrived at their hotel prior to their series with the Chicago Bulls. Oddly enough, Jim and I had no idea at the time what the hell was going on. We only knew we had to get to *our* event, which just so happened to be at the same hotel. In retrospect, I have no idea how Jim and I found a parking place that night, but we somehow parked the car and set off to the hotel, ready to entertain a large group of excited kids.

We arrived at the hotel the exact moment the team bus was pulled in. The entire area outside the hotel was roped off, and police were there to ensure the safety of all the players and coaches. Reporters from across the globe lined the entrance, and camera and satellite trucks covered entire blocks. The clicking sound of cameras, the brightness of the flashing lights, and the sound of reporters shouting questions to the players was intense. The intensity increased when head coach, Doug Collins, stepped off the bus followed by the legend himself, Michael Jordan.

With all the security in place, it was apparent nobody without proper team credentials was getting in that door. Nobody, that is, except the Bluez Brothers. Jim and I strolled up to one of the police tape lines in full costume, stepped under the Do Not Cross tape, and made our way toward the hotel. An officer was about to stop us when another, presumably his supervisor, yelled, "Hey! Jake and Elwood! How ya doin'?" Jim and I played to the crowd as if the press was there to see us. I worked the line shaking hands while Jim said, "No pictures or questions, please!" The officer who had tried to stop us laughed, assumed we were part of the festivities, and gestured towards the door. He asked us if we had credentials and Jim reached into his briefcase and pulled out a slice of white bread, while I brandished a crushed pack of cigarettes. With that, we entered the door right after Collins and Jordan.

We both mumbled and laughed quietly to each other about how freaked out we were. I told him to stay calm and keep walking before somebody figured out we weren't with the Wizards party. Rather than ask where the elevator was, we simply followed the two basketball greats when a P.R. man directed them towards one.

We assumed we would have to take the next car because generally, celebrities of that stature rode alone. Instead, the PR man waved us onto the elevator. After we, Jordan, and Collins were on board, he followed. As the door closed, he asked us what floor we needed. In a wonderful bit of coincidence, our banquet hall was located on floor "23. What did joo expect?" — For those of you who don't remember, 23 was Jordan's jersey number. That drew a laugh from everyone.

Riding that elevator was about as awkward as the elevator scene in the film starting our fictional counterparts. Everybody was silent, and all we had to entertain us was the sound of light-hearted music. I don't remember being on an elevator for so long in my life. Jim and I stood in character staring at Jordan and Collins, who stared back at us, presumably wondering who the hell booked the Blues Brothers escorts to welcome them.

Feeling the tension, I leaned towards Jordan. In a fit of nervous awe, I summoned up my comedic wit in an attempt to break the ice and said, "I bet it's pretty intimidating being on an elevator with a couple of big-name celebrities like us." Jordan leaned back and replied, "Yeah. I'll never get used to that."

Everyone laughed, and we all introduced ourselves. Jim asked, "So . . . you in town visiting family or somethin'?" After a little chit-chat, the elevator doors opened and we made our exit. Jordan told us to have a good show and I told him, "You too. Don't be nervous. There's a lot of reporters out there."

CHAPTER FIFTEEN

Bob Newhart and Bill Daily

O K, I admit it. This is more of a story about Bill Daily than it is about Bob Newhart. I never had even a single moment in the same room with Newhart. I never met him, and we didn't work together. How is it possible I have a stupid story about Bob Newhart that fits the criteria of this book? It's simple, really. Bob Newhart singlehandedly killed a gig for me. Well, maybe it was his agent, I really don't know. I only know I didn't get to work with one of my all-time comedy heroes for a ridiculous, and kind of funny, reason.

I have always been a huge fan of Newhart. Thanks to my parents, I must have listened to *The Button-Down Mind of Bob Newhart* at least a hundred times. I have seen more episodes of every damn one of his sitcoms than I can remember, and I watched the movie *Elf* because I knew he was in it. He is, and always will be, on the Mount Rushmore of comedy for me. His stories as a Chicago-area comedian were always on my mind during my days treading the boards, simply hoping for moments of genuine hilarity as great as his. I've never been able to see him perform live — likely a dreadful error of judgment and definitely an unfavorable truth of my bank account — but I've have always been a fan.

Some years back, I was still living in the Chicago suburbs and making a living as a comedian and juggler. Newhart was scheduled to appear at the Paramount Theatre in Aurora, IL; a venue I'd been trying to get in with for some time to no avail. They always had major acts coming to town, and they were good to use local acts as show openers. They also put on many local events, which could conceivably use my services, so I contacted them regularly to market my skills. I ran into the main booker of talent for the venue at a networking event, where I did my best to schmooze a little more. I was expecting the obligatory, "We have your material on file" nonsense, which was becoming a standard reply from him, but instead he asked me if I was available for a certain date. I told him I was, and he told me that Newhart would be in town and the theatre was having a difficult time finding an opening act.

"Are you kidding me? Bob Newhart? I'll do that gig for free," I told him. Just having the chance to work the same stage with him and maybe even shake his telephone dialing hand was more than enough reason to get me out of the house. The talent booker laughed and said, "Free will not be necessary. Just keep the date open." I marked the date on my calendar, and sent him a fresh press kit and video the very next day.

Later that week, I called to make sure my press materials arrived safely and continued to do the requisite schmoozing. The postman did his job well, and everything looked good for me. I was told to expect a call. I waited by the phone to hear a *yay* or *nay* from the theatre.

When the call from the theater finally came, I answered it faster than a teenaged boy when a girl calls. "Andy," said my new best friend, the talent booker. "I'm so sorry to keep you on the hook for this one, but it looks like we can't use you for the Newhart show." While being quite used to rejection in the entertainment business, I found something unusual about this particular dismissal. "*Can't* use me?" I asked. My now least favorite person replied, "Yeah. It's strange. We all looked at your material and loved it. We showed it to him [*I have no idea if he meant Newhart or the agent. My broken heart assumes he meant Newhart*] and it seems Bob doesn't like to have a juggling act go on before him. He doesn't think the audience will laugh at his act if a juggler goes on first." That was that.

I was very polite in my response, and tried to be as understanding as humanly possible. I mean, this was not the first really cool gig I didn't land. However, in my mind I was screaming, "What the holy hell? Who in the God damned world would pay good money to see Bob fucking Newhart and laugh more at me than at him? This guy is one of the last old-school comedians on the planet still capable of filling the biggest venues, and has the widest-spanning generation of hard-wired fans. He. Is. A. *Legend!* He'd get a standing ovation just for walking onstage. He could fart on his stool, and as long as he was 'making a phone call', he'd get ten minutes of belly laughs! *He* can't have a juggler open for *him*?" At least that's how I recall my inner monologue. There may have been a few more swear words in there.

This is an excuse I've heard a million times from other comedians in my travels. Nobody wants to follow a juggler, a magician, a musical comedy act, a prop comedy act or any other comedy act that involves a skill other than saying funny things, or saying things funny, into a microphone. I've had many headlining comedians at clubs ask me not to do so much juggling because otherwise their acts wouldn't do well. I used to make a joke about it. "Is your material *that* bad?" That usually didn't go over well. I began telling these folks to find solace in the fact that they were getting paid better than I was for the night, and if it bothered them so much they should write a 45-minute set about how much jugglers suck ass. A fellow juggler, Michael Goudeau, summed it up best. I'll paraphrase: Comedians have to entertain a crowd with stories about things that happened already. Jugglers entertain crowds with things they're going to do for the audience before their very eyes. "Here's what I am going to do for *you*" as opposed to "Here's what happened to *me*." Even knowing this, I was upset that this was the reason I would not be opening up for Bob Newhart. Even though this had happened to me with so many other working comics, it seemed strange that an established act like Bob Newhart would worry about such a thing. I mean, *nobody* would have paid the ticket price to see me. They would all be there to see him and I'd be the guy pissing off the crowd simply by *not* being

Bob Newhart. Being an opening act can always be a little disconcerting. Being an opening act for someone of such massive fame is truly not one for the weak. I had to know more.

A little research provided an interview with Newhart talking about one of his earliest days in the business. *Button-Down Mind* was either about to be released or had just come out and he was hitting big. At this particular show, he followed a juggling act, and as a result, Newhart bombed. He decided then that a comic simply can't compete with feats of skill, and when he got to a position in his career where he could choose his opening acts, he vowed to never have a juggler perform before him again. Decades after that incident, after the millions of albums sold, after numerous concerts, films, and hit television shows, he continued to keep the juggler ban in effect. I've always said entertainers are the most superstitious creatures of habit out there.

In retrospect, I shouldn't have been so surprised. I had, in fact, been warned by another comedy legend about Bob's hatred for all things juggling not quite a year before when I had been fortunate to meet another comedy hero of mine, Mr. Bill Daily. You should remember Daily from his roles on *I Dream of Jeannie* and *The Bob Newhart Show*. If not, for the love of God, watch some classic television! While many people don't immediately think of Bill Daily as any kind of comedy legend, he truly is a master and his performances should be watched very closely. His comedic timing and ability to take the most mundane lines and transform them into comedy gold is unparalleled. In short, he is a genius. My father was always keen to point out to me how undeniably funny Daily was on TV. With great reverence, both dad and I would watch him hold his own with Newhart, and he often stole the scene.

Long before his noteworthy television roles made him famous, Daily was a hard-working stand-up comedian working the road in night clubs, theatres, and other venues. He was a great friend of Bob Newhart's, and essentially cut his teeth with Bob on many stages throughout Chicago and across the country. There weren't many comedy clubs around in his day, so he performed in some really rough rooms.

I met Mr. Daily at a Hollywood collector's show where I was working as a cameraman for a friend of mine with a cable access show. The host of the show was also a stand-up comedian. While he was scouring the show for celebrities to interview, he didn't immediately head to Daily's table. I was rather insistent *this* was the guy to speak to, particularly for fans of great comedy. We managed to interview Daily, and he was very generous with his time. He rattled off some great stories about his days on the road with Newhart, comedy theory, his iconic television roles, and his life in show business.

Later, he and I got some one-on-one time together and he shared fantastic tales of nights when both he and Newhart bombed on stage. We both laughed about how awful it feels to stand onstage with no audience laughter or applause. I am fascinated with stories from entertainers of all kinds about the nights they tanked. I've always believed you can only learn a few things from a great show, but you can learn a wealth of things from an awful show. You simply don't get better at your craft if you don't suffer the indignity of failing so publicly on stage. These tales are the common denominator in the performing arts. Bombing is the great equalizer, and the best way to humble an ego.

I asked Daily if there was one particular night they bombed that that stood out in his mind. He smiled and said, "Well I remember a night where I did all right, but Bob really fell flat. He had to follow a variety act. A juggler. Man, he hates having to follow a juggler."

I simply couldn't stop laughing as he continued the story. Mr. Daily knew I was in the business and performed comedy across the country, but he was unaware I was also a juggler. When I told him, he laughed and said, "God, I hope you never have to work with Bob!"

CHAPTER SIXTEEN

Malcolm McDowell
and Robert Altman

L egendary film director, Robert Altman, has made some of the most acclaimed and entertaining movies. He also made *The Company*, a rather forgettable and extremely slow-paced film about Chicago's very own Joffrey Ballet Company. *The Company* was released in 2003, and starred Neve Campbell, James Franco, and Malcolm McDowell. It was shot almost exclusively in Chicago, which meant a lot of work for Chicago actors and production assistants. I know some people, mostly dancers, who loved this film. The general populace, however, almost universally stayed *far* away from any theatre running the film. *I* didn't even go see this movie in the theatre, and I was *in* the damned thing. Yes, I was an extra in this film, but let me assure you, it was not by choice. I rarely took any work as an extra after deciding that, while I loved acting, I hated being around actors.

I had originally been contacted by this particular Chicago-area casting director about my comedy juggling act. She was looking for a funny act to perform at a dinner party being held for the cast and crew of *The Company*. Bear in mind, this was long before the Internet made life *easier* for people, and the majority of the people online still used a dial-up connection. High-speed Internet use was only available for a hefty price, and Ethernet cables were about as expensive as modems. I mention this because, while I had worked for her in the past, she wasn't an agent who booked comedy or variety acts so she didn't have my promotional materials. Our mutual friend, K.T. Matson — another casting director who had used me for various events and was also working on *The Company* — had recommended me for this gig. Oddly enough, K.T. didn't have any of my promotional materials either, which made me wonder why I so diligently sent out press kits and videos to so many people if they were just going to be tossed or lost. However, I had bigger fish to fry.

I needed to get my tape and other promotional materials together and delivered to her pronto if I was to land this high-profile job. Yes, I said tape. As in VHS tape. There weren't many people using DVDs at the time. Sure, I had a popular website with many videos on it, but again, not everyone had the super-fast, reasonably-priced, "I-wanna-watch-some-porn-*now*-dammit," internet we all enjoy today. The production company for this major Hollywood film had it, but sending e-mails containing large files filled with notes and dailies (raw footage of the day's shoot) took precedence over e-mails containing large files of little ole me eating fire and making people laugh. Moreover, sending the files took too damned long. So, I repeat, I needed to get my tape to this agent in a damn hurry, which proved to be a royal pain in the ass.

She needed the press kit and information that night or the following morning, and I had a full day of gigs planned. Her schedule made taking this package to her office during the few moments that were both convenient and possible for me impossible. To make matters worse, I didn't have a tape to spare; dubbing decks were also freaking expensive. As an added bonus, I lived in a far off Chicago suburb. Any of the locations where I could deliver this package were in the heart of the city. That made the delivery of said package dependent upon perfect traffic conditions, which never happen during daylight hours in Chicagoland.

I wanted this job, if only to meet Altman or McDowell, so I made it work. The money wasn't bad either. I finished the last of my gigs, and finally received a message from her on my *answering machine* with an address where I could deliver the tape. After a long day of shows, little rest, some fancy editing, and the clever use of multiple VHS players, I had a tape and other Andy-centric propaganda ready to go. I made the trip into the city, dealt with evening traffic, and dumped my tape off at an office location. I had been told that there would be someone at the office to receive the package. There was not. After making a few calls and getting no answers, I crammed the package into the mail slot on the office door, and was relieved to find it just barely fit. I left a message for the agent letting her know that the tape was now in her possession and hoped for the best.

A few days went by, including the day of the event they were so certain I would be working. I was disappointed, but nobody could say I didn't try to land this job. I assumed it was a dead issue. The day after the event, I received a call from K.T. Matson. She had the other casting director with her, and they both thanked me profusely for jumping through hoops to get them my materials. They also apologized for not booking me. I had never received an apology for *not* getting a gig before. I told them it was no big deal, these things happen — the usual things I say when trying to be gracious and stay in good graces with someone.

It turns out that she had indeed presented my material, and that I had been in contention for the gig, but they ended up booking a comedienne instead at the recommendation of someone on the local crew. I was assured the comedienne had not been the casting director's choice, and that the lady who performed that evening was crass, unfunny, and offended most everyone in the room, including Robert Altman.

"How the hell do you offend Robert Altman?" I thought. He was something of a rebel from day one, and was not adverse to using some colorful language and portraying rather indelicate things on camera. "You've gotta get up pretty early to put in that kind of effort," I joked. K.T. laughed and said, "Now *that's* funny. Way funnier than what we heard last night." Given that it wasn't that good of a joke, I believe the comedienne really *was* awful.

K.T. told me they felt so bad about all the trouble I went through to get them my promotional materials and still not getting the job, they wanted to make it up to me by getting me some work on set as an extra. I told her it really wasn't necessary, but she was rather insistent I show up. Having nothing planned for the next day, I decided to take the job, make my whopping $50, and eat all the donuts or sandwiches I could eat to be able to say I was in a Robert Altman film.

Wardrobe in hand, I showed up ridiculously early in the morning as per protocol when on a film set. I knew, also per protocol, that it was unlikely I would be called to do any actual work for about five or six hours. I hadn't bothered to bring a book since I had plenty of business calls to make, people to meet, and a lot of people-watching ahead of me. Besides, I could play *Snake* on my Nokia cell phone for *hours* and never get bored. How many dated references can I make in one chapter?

I have said this many times. If you have ever dreamed about getting paid to do nothing, work as an extra in television and films. The majority of your day will be spent, eating, reading, chatting, and primarily waiting to be called into place. You won't make great money at it, but you could make steady money as a background performer if you're independently wealthy, I suppose.

Since it had been a long time since I had done any sort of extra work, this was very entertaining for me. I spent more time watching people I have decided to call *career extras* chat about their non-existent lives in films and act important than I actually did on set. These folks are mostly retirees looking for ways to fill their time, or one-half of a couple where somebody works and the other one is an extra in movies. Anyone who has done acting regularly has seen these people. I'm not being shallow, I'm telling you the career extras are out there, and they are both frightening and entertaining at once. One woman actually wrote a book about her long and successful career as an extra and brought copies to sell to anyone she didn't recognize from other shoots. I'm guessing she made more money off of newbie actors hoping to get real insight on how to make it in the biz then she ever did as an extra. There was even a chapter on how to maximize your time at the craft services table. I kid you not.

I listened to these people ramble on about their scenes with Jack (Nicholson), Robert (DeNiro), and Clint (Eastwood), referring to them by their first names and acting as if they were best of friends working out some critical dialogue on screen. More often than not, I was certain pretending to be friends with Costner — I'm sorry, *Kevin* — was the only acting these people had ever done. Listening to these ridiculous exchanges may have been what inspired me to do something on set worthy of repeating here.

Eventually, our one and only scene was finished being lit, and we were all called to the set. The scene was a formal banquet and most of the extras were playing either dignitaries at the main table or esteemed guests at round banquet tables. I was an esteemed guest. By this point in the day, I had heard every lame story from every vapid wannabe entertainer in the room and took it upon myself to be a bit of a smartass in conversation after we were seated. Mostly for levity's sake, but partially to ruffle the feathers of these hard-core *actors*.

After hearing story after story about *the craft*, and all the blathering about favorite movies and the major stars these folks had worked with, I couldn't help but take great pleasure in realizing not one of these self-appointed acting experts noticed when a true film heavy-hitter and immediately recognizable celebrity, Malcolm McDowell, entered the room. My whole table, if not the whole room just went about their business, cackling on about the impressive and powerful actors they have worked with over the years with wild-eyed exuberance. I ended up interrupting one woman (I think she was the one who wrote the book) and said, "Well, if you're all that interested in big stars, Malcolm McDowell just walked in."

Everyone at the table shut up and began shooting glances in every direction. Heads turned and craned every which way in the hopes they would see McDowell. With all of these film buffs in the room, all of these "serious actors" at my table, and all of these celebrity stalkers around me, not *one* person recognized McDowell. I had to point him out to everyone at the table. As one, they let out an "Ohhhhhhh!" It was absolutely ridiculous.

Soon thereafter, Academy Award-nominated director, Robert Altman, came into the room. Again, none of the world's experts on the film industry sitting at my table noticed him. I chose to shut up and just watch to see what the genius director had to say, hoping to get a little insight into the way a film is made.

What struck me about Altman was an imposing, but very approachable, presence about him. When he and McDowell were standing together discussing the scene, there was a genuine energy that only comes from those moments you know you'll never see again. These were two true stars in Hollywood, and they were right there working on a simple scene which took five hours to set up. It was very cool to say the least.

An even better trait I was fortunate enough to witness was Altman's sense of humor at work. At my table, we were all asked to get back up so a few changes could be made. The director wanted set pieces moved to better fit within the shot he envisioned. He pointed with his finger to a spot along the banquet table where he wanted a chair relocated. When the crew member moved the chair towards Altman's finger, it seemed to get caught between the chair and the table. Altman yelped in pain. Everyone assumed that his finger had been pinched between the chair and the table's edge, which startled the room and panicked the crew. As Altman shook his finger in reactive pain, blowing on it and sucking in air through his teeth, the local crewman, now worried he'd just lost his job for hurting an Academy Award-nominated director, rushed to lend aid. As soon as the crewman got close enough to help, Altman smiled. He tussled the crewman's hair as he laughed and said, "Gotcha!" Everyone got a good laugh, and I loved watching Altman's smile turn to a wicked grin of delight.

After the fake injury played out, Mr. Altman started taking a good look at all of the extras in the room, truly seeing every face. He immediately turned to one of the production assistants and asked why so many wonderful faces were not better placed so he could get a few shots with character during McDowell's upcoming speech. Soon, he was pointing to specific people and asking them to move to new places. I was standing next to McDowell at the time, and trying desperately to find a way to start a conversation so I could tell him I was a fan of his work. Then it dawned on me: Malcolm McDowell is one of those actors who has done so many well-known cult films (*A Clockwork Orange, Caligula*) that he probably has a creepy fan base, and has likely had many people walk up to him in white shirts and suspenders, talking about the great Ludwig Van. He probably never wants to hear *anyone* say to him, "I really admire your work" again. I chose to simply marvel at how much taller he was than I had expected and leave him alone. Thinking about it now, this chapter should really be called *Robert Altman.*

Turns out, it was a good thing I didn't say anything to McDowell, as Altman was giving a little pep talk to the extras, describing the scene so we could all act accordingly. Moreover, while rearranging the extras, he decided he wanted a particularly tight shot of someone's face watching McDowell's speech. That meant an on-the-spot reworking of a specific camera angle. As the camera and lights were adjusted, he asked me if I would mind moving from my table and heading to this new filming destination.

"No problem, Bob," I replied. A few laughs aside, the room became silent and several extras nearly passed out from shock. I simply smirked, looking rather sly in my tuxedo.

Mr. Altman cocked his head and asked, "Did you just call me Bob?"

"Yes I did, Bob. That is your name, right?"

Not missing a beat, Mr. Altman said, "It certainly is. And what should I call you?"

With a nod and a wink, I said, "Bob, you may call me Mr. Martello." A bit more laughter raked through the room.

Altman smiled and said, "Well, Mr. Martello, would you please take your mark?"

"Sure thing, Bob," I said, and took my seat.

We shot the scene a handful of times with modest variations on the dialogue, as you would expect from an Altman film. A few different camera angles and a few sips of fake wine later we were finished. The cameraman in charge of my tight close up shook my hand and told me I did very well at not overacting in the scene. Apparently, when the camera is so tight on one's face, even the smallest movement looks *huge* on the big screen. I could now add "doesn't overact during close-ups" to my growing resume. I could now also add that I was in a Robert Altman film; something my father in particular would have been proud to know.

As the actors and crew dispersed, I took a moment to introduce myself to the famous director, being certain to address him as Mr. Altman this time. As I shook his hand, I apologized for my jerky behavior. I told him about some of the films my dad had me watch as an introduction to his work, how I was very much a fan, and that it truly was an honor to watch him in action. Mr. Altman simply smiled, thanked me for my work that day, and said, "Mr. Martello, it has been my distinct pleasure."

CHAPTER SEVENTEEN

Anthony Anderson

If you go on YouTube and do a search for "plate spinning" (and why wouldn't you, really?), you will very likely find a few entries from yours truly. One such video will surely pique your interest. It features me with comedian and acclaimed actor, Anthony Anderson, on *The WGN Morning News*. At the time of this writing, this clip has nearly 40,000 views, and will very likely be the only clip of mine to reach such success. Unless you really want to see me get beaten up in an alley. That's there too.

Having appeared on *The Bozo Show* several times, I was contacted by Jeff Hoover of *The WGN Morning News* to perform some plate-spinning on the show. That program is a fabulous mix of news and nonsense. With Hoover at the helm and Bozo long off the air, he had the notion to contact as many people as possible who had appeared on the iconic show to recreate some of that television magic. Anthony Anderson was also a scheduled guest. He was there to promote his sitcom, *All About the Andersons*. You may recognize him from films like *Hustle and Flow*, or television shows like *The Shield*, and *Black-ish*.

He is a modern-day "That Guy" actor. You know, that actor you have seen a million times, the one who's in *everything*, but you can never remember his name. Even in starring roles, it's difficult for people to immediately remember his name. You remember his sometimes award-nominated performances from film and television, but he's just "that guy". As far as I'm concerned, Anthony Anderson is that guy. I wouldn't be a bit surprised if you are actually looking him up online right now. Admit it, you are! I think being a "That Guy" actor is the best thing to be. You never stop working, your work is loved by millions, you live in a nice home, and you never have to worry about too many people bothering you at restaurants or snapping your photo. God bless the Jeffery Tambors, the Edie McClurgs and the Anthony Andersons of show business.

Aside from his skills as an actor, Anderson is a talented comedian. His affable nature and ability to make any situation a fun experience makes him a favorite on set and as a guest on talk shows and news programs. This skill with people and a knack for making a scene uniquely his was put to good use on this particular show.

His segment came before mine, but we both had to be there ridiculously early; like when I shot episodes of *The Bozo Show.* I found myself in the same studio, on the same stage, at the same ungodly hour. I didn't have any items to steal from the set, but I did have time to chat with Anderson about his comedy, his show, and how awful it is for people like us to be awake that early.

Because he was essentially trapped there, and certainly tired from the early hour, he made it a point to take full control of the WGN set. Sometimes those exhausted, dreamlike moments in a comedian's head produce actions and comedy which can only be fueled by a sort of sleepwalking adrenaline. He not only made his appearance and promoted his show well, but he insinuated himself into many segments: ordering a pizza on the news phone as they came out of a break, horsing around with some of my juggling props, and making sure everyone knew this funny man was in town.

As my segment with WGN's Paul Konrad began, I made certain comedic nonsense would ensue. I was going to teach Konrad how to spin plates on the air, and he was insistent during rehearsal that he have no knowledge of how to perform the task before filming. Within minutes, plates were falling left and right, and throughout our discussion of the Bozo days, we made certain to achieve a level of general mayhem in the studio where I had performed the same plate routine many years earlier. When the two-minute mark approached, with only a minute or so left in the piece, Anderson stormed on set. What Konrad didn't know was that I had taught Anderson the basics of plate-spinning earlier. He brought an extra bit of levity, excitement, and showmanship to the segment. Many plates were destroyed, and belly laughs were had. After all was said and done, we had a fantastic, high-energy moment on the show . . . and I ended up with a very popular YouTube clip. I wonder how many people have looked Anderson up and found him spinning plates on an early morning show in Chicago. Moreover, I wonder how many of his hard core fans, the ones who *do* know his name, watch the clip and think, "Who the hell is that guy spinning plates with to Anthony Anderson?"

CHAPTER EIGHTEEN

Gladys Knight and a Pip

I learned the plate-spinning act out of necessity; I never intended for it to become a mainstay in my comedy and juggling routine. I figured that act was old as the hills, didn't seem to require any skill, and everybody had seen it a million times before. I was only right about it being an old act. As it happened, it may not take a lot of skill to get ten plates spinning on poles, but it takes a tremendous amount to make the act seem difficult, exciting, and filled with comedic tension.

While touring the Midwest with Family Showcase Theater — a small circus owned by the Reynolds family of Mt. Vernon, Illinois — I was informed a few hours before a show that Gary Noel had broken his foot and leg. Gary, a mainstay of this particular circus, performed many acts on the program, among them was a plate-spinning act. Panicked, the show owners asked the rest of us if we had any other acts or if we could at least pad our existing acts a bit to offset the time lost by Noel's absence.

This was one of my first times working a full tour with the show, and I was as green as it gets. I knew there were some in the family who were not all that happy with the new guy, but I made a big impression on them when I told them I had plenty more in my bag of tricks. I had already been doing hour-long shows as a solo act, but I was only performing two, seven-minute spots for them. I had everything with me, and put together a couple other segments. They asked if I would be able to do a plate-spinning act since that was in the pre-printed programs. I had never done one before, but I was familiar with the prop plates sold at juggling and magic shops around the country. I thought, "How hard could it be?" The answer proved to be, "Very damn hard" because Gary was not using perfectly-balanced, aluminum plates with a point in the middle of them. He was using actual china dinnerware found at thrift stores around the

United States. It may not seem like a big deal to you, but if you've never done the act before, it was a hell of a big deal. Gary taught me the basics from his chair and walked me through the routine a few times. I felt I had the gist of it. He leant me his wardrobe and props, and that night, with barely 30 minutes of training, I went into the ring and attempted to spin six measly plates.

Let me say, I was more nervous than I have ever been in my life. I simply was not one to go out on stage and attempt an act without countless hours of practice. I knew the show must go on, and the sponsors expected a 90-minute show from us, so I went out there. By this point, I had helped set up the show, performed four different types of juggling acts, and sold balloons and coloring books at intermission. I was not only exhausted, I was petrified the act wouldn't go over. Thankfully, it ended up being the single funniest plate-spinning act in circus history. The crowd went absolutely crazy with laughter. The sponsors were very happy. Even the band had a hard time keeping their composure. I don't think I have ever received a larger ovation of applause and laughter in my career.

None of this had anything to do with my years of juggling skills, my well-honed comedic timing, or my natural ability as a plate-spinner. They were laughing because I broke every damn plate Gary had that night! The closest I came to completing my task was 5 plates. The circus ring was a disaster area filled with broken porcelain, stoneware, and enamel. It was absolutely hilarious to watch, and everyone loved this genuine moment of embarrassment for me.

By the next show, we had restocked the plates, I practiced more before the show, and I did the act properly. I finished the tour with more money in my pocket, a newfound respect from the show owners for stepping up for them, and I had a new act. Gary even built me my own plate rack to use in case I wanted to book the act myself.

Back home, on a whim, I brought it to one of my school shows specifically because they wanted some true circus acts and not just a guy who could juggle. The act went over like gangbusters and, after trying it out at a few different places, I decided it would be the finale to my full-length stage show from then on. It wasn't long before I performed it on *The Bozo Show* in Chicago and started marketing it to talent agents. Soon, it was *the* reason I was getting calls. I have performed that act for national television commercials, and before crazed fans of the Insane Clown Posse. I even turned it into a corporate training seminar, booking the act for top dollar with Coca-Cola, Boeing, Bridgestone/Firestone, and Harley-Davidson, among others.

Like I said, I never thought I would use that act again, let alone that it would generate a big part of my career's identity and put a lot more money in my bank account. I certainly never expected that played-out old act would put me on the same stage as the supremely talented Gladys Knight.

In late May of 2007, I made the move from Chicago to Las Vegas for reasons that belong in a different book. Moving to Vegas was one of the most exciting and most terrifying things I had ever done. I'd always wanted to live there, but wanted to do it "the right way": meaning I would have established contacts and agents, and would simply start working as an entertainer the same way I had been doing in Chicago for well over 20 years. The reality was that I had very little work lined up, and the circumstances which led me to Vegas were immediate, which left me with little time to think or plan.

While I was able to get a gig here and there, I was not working often enough to cover the bills. I took on full-time work at a local chain of magic shops. I loved and hated the job all at once, but it did keep me busy and my bills paid. A big reason for taking the job was the owners. They knew I was a performer, and they very graciously allowed me time off whenever I had a booking so long as I gave them advance notice. This was extremely helpful when I was contacted by an event planning company in late August of 2007. They had found my website, and were desperate to find a plate-spinning act for a corporate event in West Virginia that October.

I was extremely hopeful and anxious for this event to come in. It wasn't work in Vegas, but the paycheck would take care of quite a few bills. I spoke to the event planner, who was already impressed with my resume and my website, sent out additional promotional materials, and offered up a quote.

Pricing an act has always been a bit of a mystery to me. I always want the best amount, but also know everybody needs to not only be happy with the act, but everybody needs to be happy with the money spent and the markup for the company booking me. Like any entertainer, I also did not want money to be the reason I was excluded from consideration. Over the years, I learned to ask a lot of questions before giving a price, even though that's usually the first thing anyone asks about. In this case, I knew the location (West Virginia), but I also needed to know the type of event, how much work I would be doing, the type of client I would be performing for, and who else was there. Knowing it was on the eastern part of the States, I had already come up with a base price that factored in flight and accommodations. When

I heard the location was the historic Greenbrier Resort and the headliner was the one and only Gladys Knight, I realized I could shoot for the stars, but would settle for the moon.

The Greenbrier, also known as America's Resort, has been serving high-profile guests on its pristine and elegant property since 1778. Located in White Sulphur Springs, West Virginia, it's an absolute palace by every definition of the word. I do not recall too many places more beautiful than White Sulphur Springs and the Greenbrier. Knowing the venue location and that the end company was ponying up the dough to have Gladys Knight perform told me they had the cash I wanted. We settled on a price everybody could live with, although, I admit that I quoted a slightly lower price just so I could see Knight sing. I mean, really. Who wouldn't want to say they got paid to hear Gladys Knight?

The only real *problem* with taking this event was the timing. I had already purchased tickets for that weekend to see The Killer, Jerry Lee Lewis, perform in Primm, Nevada. He wasn't performing many concerts anymore, and I'd never gotten the chance to see him before. This may be my only chance, but . . . Gladys Knight . . . all that cash . . .

I was also scheduled to speak at the 110th birthday celebration of Searchlight, Nevada that weekend. The long-gone El Rey Club — the subject of my first book — had been located in Searchlight. While the book was far from becoming a reality at that point, I had been invited to discuss the history of the place, meet many of the long-time locals, and maybe get more interview subjects for the book project. It was a golden opportunity for me, and I truly wanted to be there, but . . . Gladys Knight . . . all that cash . . .

Cooler heads, and a big stack of bills, prevailed. I took the event, my younger brother flew in from the Midwest to use my ticket to see Jerry Lee, and the town of Searchlight got a couple of great speakers to replace me; both of whom I had recommended.

I knew I had made the right call as soon as I arrived at the resort; this place was *posh!* The butlers had butlers. The food was incredible, the landscape was breathtaking, and the rooms were far nicer than any I'd stayed in previously, and I got to stay for a full weekend.

We spent one whole day rehearsing every little detail of the performance. Well, every detail except Knight's performance. She wasn't scheduled to be there until the day of the show. There was a special rehearsal and sound check planned just for her and her incredible band. Everyone was rather pleasant to work with, and I was treated well. I guess having a plate-spinner was a big part of the show, and I am, after all, the last great plate-spinner.

By show-time, I was most pleased with the entire experience thus far. Frankly, I was also so damned happy to be working as an entertainer again it felt like I had new life in my old bones. I took the stage and began my act. By this point in my career, any broken plates were for comedic effect and not because I was a total moron. The crowd laughed at all the right places and the response was exactly what the client wanted, if not what I had grown accustomed to. What I was not expecting to see was a door on the side of the room opening up so Gladys Knight herself could watch my act.

She peered out after hearing a plate-spinner was going to perform and watched every single second. Her brilliant white smile seemed to provide extra stage lighting for me, and I began to feel like I was performing for her alone. I cannot say if that was the best single performance of my routine I had ever done, but I can say I don't remember a time where I was happier to be presenting that old chestnut of an act.

When Miss Knight started her set, I watched every damned minute. She was a delight to see and hear. Such a beautiful, pristine voice coming through those speakers. There was not a soul in the room who didn't love hearing this Motown legend sing and interact with her brother, Bubba Knight, who was one of the original Pips. She made us laugh with off-the-cuff remarks and some planned comedy. She made us sing along with every note, and brought the house down.

A highlight for me came in the middle of her set. She began to talk about all of the great acts who had appeared on the stage before her "Did you all see that plate-spinner? That was so amazing! I haven't seen one in years. When I heard we were having a plate-spinner, I had to watch." I hadn't expecting her to call me out specifically, so I was touched when she mentioned it. She caught a glimpse of me in the audience, and gestured in my direction. The crowd gave me a little extra applause. If nothing else, I knew my client was pleased.

After the show, I wanted so badly to meet her and tell her how much I appreciated her wonderful career and the shout-out. She was being so gracious and attentive to the bigwigs from the group that I didn't want to bother her. She was truly a graceful, wonderful lady who took time to shake every hand and pose for every photo. I was close enough to touch her, but I decided this would be one more time I let the moment be the real memory and let her do her thing.

Instead, I started up a conversation with her brother, Bubba. He made a point to tell me how much he loved my act, but the real reason he had come over talk to me was because of my shoes. He was wearing a wonderful pair of spectator wingtips, and was desperate to know where I had gotten my black-and-white flame-pattered shoes. We ended up talking about stage footwear for a *very* long time. We compared notes about the business, shared a few road stories, and he even taught me a few Pip dance moves; moves that I can't perform with any alacrity to this day.

In all, my trip to White Sulphur Springs was nothing less than a success. I'm still a bit upset at the agent who promised to get me video of the show and never did, but I can forgive most anything so long as the paycheck clears. The real pleasures were seeing Gladys Knight bust out "Midnight Train to Georgia", having the privilege of opening for her, and talking spectators with Bubba. All because a plate-spinner from a little-known family-owned circus broke his foot three hours before a show in a tiny Midwestern town. Who'd have guessed?

CHAPTER NINETEEN

Tony Curtis

I absolutely love living in Las Vegas. The list of things I find so much better about living here as opposed to living in the Midwest gets longer every day. I love the weather, I adore the scenery, and I cherish the fact I have not seen a mosquito in years. Even though Vegas has lost a lot of its credibility as the Entertainment Capital of the world, and you don't see as many big name acts with residencies on the Strip anymore, Las Vegas is a place full of entertainers: some big name acts, legendary stars, and people who can only be called Vegas Famous. As a result of living in Vegas, I have been fortunate enough to meet, work with, or make friends with people like The Amazing Jonathan, Steve Rossi, Louie Anderson, Pia Zadora, The Smothers Brothers, James

Cromwell, Penn & Teller, Lance Burton, Drew, Carey, Marie Osmond, and many others.

When I first moved out here, I often made the joke that if you lived in Las Vegas long enough, you would eventually meet Tony Curtis. Curtis was both a long-time resident of Las Vegas, and a very present member of the community. I've had several conversations with Las Vegans with stories about hanging out with Curtis.

Early on in my residency in Las Vegas, I found myself at an antique mall with my then-wife, April. There was a booth closing up permanently, and they were selling many of their items at 50% off. Among them was a cool looking ticket for a drive-in theater in Monroeville, California. This was more than just a ticket; it was a piece of Vegas-themed memorabilia suitable for framing. The ticket was for a film called *40 Pounds of Trouble*, a comedy starring Phil Silvers, Suzanne Pleshette, a five-year-old Claire Wilcox, and *the* Tony Curtis. What caught my eye was the very long ticket festooned with movie artwork. Attached to the ticket was a series of tear-away playing cards featuring the four main actors as the aces. It was a clever marketing tool, and I snatched it up immediately for the low price of $7.50. I joked with April and the clerk that I wanted it for that fateful moment when I, like any Vegas resident, got my obligatory meeting with Tony Curtis. "I'll get him to sign this for me. It's part of his duties as the resident Tony Curtis of Las Vegas." I never expected my joke to become a reality.

There's a wonderful organization affectionately known as the Las Vegas Old Timers' Media Group that was started by a bunch of retired Las Vegans with a common background in the local media. They decided to get together for lunch and talk about what the town used to be like. The group now meets monthly, and has become a great meeting place for Vegas locals and retirees of all backgrounds to share a wealth of wonderful stories about the rich and textured history of Las Vegas. I used to attend regular luncheons while researching my first book, *The King of Casinos*. The group always has a tasty lunch, great conversation, raffles, and a guest speaker.

One night while sharing drinks and watching baseball with friend, and fellow Media Group attendee, Rich Friedland, I was presented with the opportunity to emcee the luncheon. Rich was the regular emcee at the time, and he was going to be out of town for the next meeting. Being an entertainer and familiar with the group, he thought I would be a suitable replacement.

"There's one thing I should tell you," Rich said. "But you have to keep this to yourself since it would be kind of a surprise." I was all ears at this point. "You know we always have a guest speaker, right?" I nodded. "There's about a 90% chance the speaker that day will be Tony Curtis." I immediately started laughing because just that day I had made my "live here long enough and you meet Tony Curtis" joke to a friend admiring my *40 Pounds of Trouble* ticket. Rich went on to say that Curtis wasn't confirmed, and that there would be an alternate speaker lined up in case Mr. Curtis couldn't attend. In my head I *knew* he would be there; it fell well into the wonderful serendipity of my frequently enjoyable, surprising life.

On Monday, June 21, 2010, I headed to the banquet hall to emcee the luncheon. I still had no confirmation Mr. Curtis would be there, but I figured I would still be enjoying a great lunch with some fun people. By kick off time for the luncheon, I had received confirmation from Lisa Giola-Acres, the unofficial head of the group, we were indeed going to be having lunch with a legend.

As the attendees shuffled into the venue and paid for their lunch, I noticed a tall man pushing another man in a wheelchair. The man in the chair was wearing all white, including his cowboy hat. While most wouldn't have known at a glance, I knew Tony Curtis was riding in that chair. To me, even at 85, without his hairpiece, and seemingly a little frail from health issues, there was no mistaking the familiar face of an icon.

The man wheeling Curtis around was Gene Kilroy, a life-long friend of Mr. Curtis who was always on-hand for him at events like these. He wheeled the star into the room, and looked around for someone who seemed to be in charge of the event. I suppose I looked like the guy in charge, because he approached me. Pointing to Curtis, he said, "Uhh . . . Tony Curtis?" I smiled at Kilroy and said, "Yeah. I've heard of him." The Hollywood legend peered up at me from under his white hat and offered that all-too-recognizable smile and a wink. He got the joke. I directed them both to some of the more official members of the group who got them settled at a table with some lunch.

I was quite taken aback by how, at this stage in his life, he looked very much like a combination of Carl Reiner and my father: bald, an inviting and smiling face, a well-kept moustache, and Van Dyke beard. There was a commanding presence about him, even in his some-what withered state. I learned that he could still walk, but after a bout of pneumonia the previous year he spent more time off of his feet than on them. It was interesting to see all of the identifying features of a Hollywood star combined with the frailty of age. It had also been many years since anyone had reminded me of my dead father in such a way.

What astounded me most was seeing how many long-time Las Vegans and people in his age group failed to recognize Curtis. Much like when I had watched all of the so-called actors miss Malcolm MacDowell on a movie set, Curtis was just a guy in the room to the majority of these people. Tony Curtis was from an era where there were only three very new television networks, no internet or cable TV, tons of movie theaters, and a level of fame so great, everyone would recognize you. To see so few even pay attention to him made me a little sad. Although, I was comforted knowing the surprise guest speaker was indeed going to be a surprise.

Being the emcee had its privileges. I was lucky enough to be seated at the same table as Curtis and Kilroy. I sat quietly and let other people ask him questions and chat with him. After a while, he very kindly asked me a few questions about what I did for a living. At that time, I was in a headlining comedy and magic show on Fremont Street, which delighted him. Being a magician himself, the conversation at the table quickly became one between just the two of us.

Hoping he would actually be there that afternoon, I had brought my *40 Pounds of Trouble* ticket with me. At a break in our conversation, others at the table began to speak with him again. I quietly approached Kilroy and asked if Mr. Curtis still signed autographs. I'm not much of an autograph guy, but I couldn't resist asking. When would I get another chance like this? At the very least, I'd hoped I could show Curtis the ticket and get him to tell a few stories about the film. I showed Kilroy what I had, and told him my silly story about how "everybody in Vegas meets Tony Curtis" which made him laugh. He got Tony's attention. When he showed him the ticket, Tony's face lit up. "My goodness, where do you get *this?*" he asked. I told him the story about the antique store and why I had bought it, including my joke about meeting him. Gene Kilroy handed him a felt tip pen, and Tony told everyone stories about the making of the film. What I did not expect was for him to do so much more than offer an autograph and a few good memories.

For those of you not aware, Mr. Curtis spent much of his life, particularly after Hollywood, as an artist. Many of his fine works of art have been on display at some of the world's most prestigious galleries and have brought in top dollar at auction. Rather than simply scroll his name on my ticket, he began to sketch out a little scene surrounding the image of himself and his co-star. He drew a little table with wine, fruit, and all the scenery of a lunch setting, completely covering the ticket. When he was finished, he wrote above his artwork: "Andy, at last, we meet." He then signed the piece and gave it back to me, thanking me for showing it to him. I was floored! I don't remember a single story about the film or what he said. I simply stared at his perfect little scene and remember feeling so dazzled by his ability to take my little joke and turn it into a shared memory for both of us. *That* was the charm he possessed. Whether it was on screen or in person, he proved himself to be nothing less than a classy gentleman with great heart and tremendous generosity. At least, that's how he appeared to this humble nobody.

With lunch eaten, it was time for the real fun to begin. I welcomed the crowd and tried my best to get the seniors to calm down and settle in for the guest speaker. You'd be amazed how difficult it is to get a bunch of geriatrics to actually listen to anything. I took care of all the formalities and regular business of the meeting, which was not met with any amount of quiet from the crowd. When I mentioned the name of our guest speaker for the afternoon, however, everyone mysteriously decided it was time to shut the hell up. I brought Mr. Curtis to the center of the room, introduced him as "a true Hollywood legend, a gifted artist, and a true Las Vegan," and he accepted a rather loud and lengthy round of applause from the astonished crowd.

As you would imagine, Curtis had a way of charming and engaging an audience. He didn't need any sort of staging or fancy lighting, and he was every bit the showman. He regaled the crowd with many humorous anecdotes and jokes. My favorite of the bunch was: "I married every one of my co-stars, except for Jack Lemmon." He spoke very quietly, with a hushed tone most were unaccustomed to from him due mostly to not fully recovering from pneumonia in 2009. Yet, even in a room filled with restless and chatty seniors — many of whom always complained they could never hear the speaker — he didn't need a microphone.

He told stories about Hollywood, his co-stars, his affairs, his mistakes, and his relatively few regrets. He also spoke very passionately about his artwork and the joy, serenity, and fulfillment it brought to his life. He had some insightful things to say about his artwork and the artists who influenced him. It seemed he knew he was at the end of the winter of his life, and was grateful for every single minute he'd had. Listening to Mr. Curtis speak so eloquently and fondly about his life and career, I got the impression that he was genuinely saying, "Thank you"; not only to the people in the room, but in a way, to the world for supporting "this skinny Jewish kid" in his long career and helping him to enjoy what he described as "the best life."

Like a professor lecturing his students, he briefly went into a little bit of acting theory and how he had survived in the business. Wanting to get a few snapshots of the moment, and to hear him better, I moved to a different part of the room. I thought I caught movement out of the corner of my eye, so I moved to my right to get out of his way. I glanced back at the man again, seeing him much clearer this time. I was certain that I *saw* the man, and I froze. The man I saw behind me looked *exactly* like my father. I knew it couldn't be him, because he'd been dead for many years, but I *saw* him, right behind me, listening to Tony Curtis speak. When I turned around to look at the table behind me again, there was nobody there. All seats were empty and nobody had disturbed a chair, a place setting, or even a water glass. It's not uncommon to see people you knew after they've passed. Most people encounter such things in the immediate aftermath of a parent or relative passing, but his phenomena hadn't happened to me in years.

I looked around the room to see if I could find a man who resembled my father so much. I didn't, and no one could have been behind me at that moment. I smiled, held back a laugh, and turned around to see Tony Curtis in his wheelchair looking right at me. He spoke about how blessed a man is who can make a living in show business. "Like this young man here," he said as he gestured at me. It was a most amazing moment for me personally.

I had a moment to ask Mr. Curtis a question during the Q & A part of the afternoon. Rather than fully answer the question, he took time to speak directly to me about the gifts a person may have inside them; gifts which should be explored and encouraged. I got the feeling he wanted me to know how special life was, not just in general, but for someone in the arts actively pursuing his dreams.

Until now, I've only told a few people about that moment. If I'm being honest, it does sound kind of corny but it seems *that* much more important to me now. When I met Tony, I wasn't exactly living the dream. I was working a fair number of corporate events, and had a short-lived show on Fremont Street, but I wasn't making much money or feeling as accomplished in the business as I'd hoped to be by the time I turned 40 and hit my 25th anniversary as an entertainer. Thinking about that day, my dad, and the things Tony Curtis said to me, I remind myself that I am blessed. For the most part, I've made a living in show business.

With his final thank-yous said, and the proclamation that he owes a lot to the world for giving him a lifetime of fun, he accepted a standing ovation and more applause than I thought possible from such a small crowd. Given the many health issues of the crowd, a standing ovation was the greatest compliment. Afterward, he graciously posed for photographs and shook hands until every last fan had their moment.

I waited patiently for the crowd to disperse so I could get a photo of my own. I felt guilty for asking since he had already spent so much time with me, but I knew this was my only real chance to capture the moment. I humbly asked if he would take one last photo. He smiled, shook my hand, and rose from his wheelchair. I insisted he needn't stand up, and he said "It would be my honor to take a photo with you."

Tony Curtis passed away just over 3 months later on September 29, 2010. To the best of my knowledge, I have the last completed piece of artwork he ever made. It hangs on my wall to this day. I spent a lot of time thinking about my experience with him when I heard of his passing. I was reminded of a great story told by Harrison Ford that sums up Curtis and his character perfectly. Other than my own personal encounter, this is my favorite story involving Curtis. It wasn't told directly to me, mind you. Come on! I'm not *that* cool.

Harrison Ford was once told by a casting director that he would never become an actor because he didn't *look* like a movie star. The casting director pulled out an old film projector and proceeded to show Ford a scene in a grocery store. He pointed at the bag boy placing items into a sack for a customer. "See that kid? That kid is *Tony Curtis*. You can't stop looking at him because he *looks* like a movie star." Ford leaned in toward the casting director's face and said quietly, "I thought he was supposed to look like a *bag boy*." I had told Curtis this story the day we met. He laughed loudly and said, "Thank God I looked like a movie star! Otherwise I would have *been* a bag boy."

CHAPTER TWENTY

Conclusions and Confessions

The more I write down these stupid stories, the more I realize the most ridiculous part may have to do with how often these anecdotes start with: "While working as a clown" or "I had an event as a Blues Brother this one time." I *do* have stupid stories about famous people where I wasn't in some crazy costume, honest. It just seems odd to me that such relatively small parts of an otherwise large career seem to have the most lasting impact. I didn't become a clown because I had a dream to work for a circus, but because I wanted to learn a lot of performance skills in a short amount of time. Ringling Bros. made that happen. I didn't become a Blues Brothers impersonator due my rampant love for the film. I did it because Jim Bina lost his regular partner, thought I was funny, and knew I was a little portly. I also did it because the money was excellent. None of these career choices had anything to do with the prospect of meeting celebrities. I had always hoped that *I* would be the famous one, which, as we have established, hasn't happened. I chose paths which would enable me to keep working and pay the bills. Some of these paths may have taken me away from the loftier goals I had set for myself, but I will always believe my dad was right when he told me "Work is work. There is no shame in making a living." Of course, he'd never said that wearing a multicolored costume, a red nose, and standing in front of the unparalleled Queen of the Blues, Koko Taylor.

I like to think that I have led something of a blessed life thus far. While I don't have the fanciest of homes or a killer car to drive around in, I can never be anything less than grateful to have made a career in entertainment for over 30 years. It is not an easy business, and very few people make it long enough to even consider themselves a professional. This life onstage has not been all smiles and laughs, and has adversely affected almost every significant relationship in my life. There have been plenty of times I was at my wit's end and down to my last few dollars. Overall, I've had a successful career that hasn't only provided many wonderful opportunities to see the world and meet some fantastic people, but has provided me with a lifetime of memories worth sharing.

These stories are only a few of the most asked about or most enjoyed. If I remain fortunate in this life, I will continue to acquire new memories, make more lifelong friends, and have more stupid stories to tell. Working in entertainment may have prepared me to meet celebrities better than most, but I won't stop being that idiot kid who struggles for the right things to say around them. Nor will I stop being the guy who makes an awkward situation more tolerable. I am honored to have the chance to share these with you, and I hope you enjoyed them all.

Since this book is filled with stupid true stories, I think it is only fair to include a few stupid lies. Now, these are not big lies for which I would rightfully deserve a lifetime of scorn for my abhorrent propensity for spreading mistruths. No, these are not stories about fudging a tax return, cheating on a spouse, misappropriating funds donated to a charity, or lying about committing major crimes. These are the kinds of lies most everyone has told in their lifetime. These are lies which appeared on my entertainment resume.

Now, don't go saying, "Well, I wouldn't have done such a thing!" If you have held a job damn near anywhere in the world, I am certain you'd be able to mention a fib or two on your own business resume. At the very least, you've found a creative way to make your meager skills sound a lot more valuable. Wasting time on the computer for hours on end very easily becomes "Proficiency in Windows operating systems". Talking and texting to your friends all day looks much better as "Great communication skills". I imagine a prostitute looking to get off her back and into an office chair could easily translate that experience into "Excellent at building interpersonal one-on-one relationships", "Works well with others", and "Adept in cash management". Everyone has done this at one point or another. It's OK. I'm not going to tell your boss, nor am I going to judge you for it. I'm merely saying that we all blur the exact truth about our experiences and skill sets every once in a while. Entertainers are no different.

Comedian and actor Billy Crystal has famously admitted to completely making up his resume in the early days of his career. Yet, none of his lies were *technically* lies. Living in New York, he would frequently attend live tapings of all kinds of television shows. Comedy, drama, or variety show, he went to them all. His resume lies involved waiting for a specific moment in the program where there would be a lull in the dialogue or a moment of silence for dramatic effect. During that time, he would clear his throat or cough thereby making him a part of the broadcast, getting his voice on the show, and placing a new credit on his resume. When he would go to auditions, casting directors would marvel at all the big name, current television shows he had appeared on, and would take a better look at his audition than if some inexperienced kid was standing before them. Clever, right?

I too have padded my resume over the years. While I cannot claim to doctoring it in such a wonderful way as Crystal, I can say my *lies* are really just *exaggerations of the truth*. The proper wording of a simple phrase can make all the difference.

While I am not retiring from entertainment any time soon, and I certainly have not achieved a level of fame which necessarily warrants me removing these credits from my resume, I believe it adds to the fun of this book. I have been asked many times about these various credits, and it only makes sense I use this book as a way to clear the air. Besides, I don't think this book will make it to the shelves of bookstores across the country, or be widely read, so the likelihood of someone in the biz denying me a look because of these confessions is pretty slim.

I mentioned one great example of such a lie earlier in this book. For many years, particularly the years Phil Collins was on every radio station's play list, my brochures and resume said that I was a "supporting act" for the British pop star. The implication being that I took the stage before Collins, who appeared at a major concert venue, and showcased my high quality act. In reality I was strolling entertainment for a Sears' event where he performed, and was well in front of the stage. However, I *did* perform at this event, and performed before Phil Collins made his appearance, so it wasn't a stretch to say I opened for Collins. Other incarnations of this resume misdirection said I had "appeared with" Collins. Which is a bit more accurate since we were on the same bill, but still not the same definition any entertainment booker would have. In fact, there was no printed bill to appear on, so even that is still somewhat of a lie. See how this works? If anyone had a right to claim he opened for Collins that day, it was this lone bagpipe player who was rattling off a long and intricate number when Collins snuck up behind him and got the crowd to cheer even more. Collins surprised the player, helped him get a well-deserved round of applause, and then sat at the piano to sing three songs before thanking Sears for sponsoring the U.S. leg of his world tour.

I've "opened for" or "appeared with" Cheap Trick, Blues Traveler, Outkast, Moby, and countless other big name stars. They were all public shows attended by thousands of people, and I was definitely booked at the same event. However, for at least the acts mentioned above, I was not on stage before them; I was merely at an event they were also playing. Cheap Trick was on stage at a family event at Great Lakes Naval Base and I appeared on a separate stage near them. Blues Traveler was the main act at the Comcast employee party at the Park West in Chicago where I was a strolling Blues Brother. Outkast and Moby were the name acts at the Area One Festival at the World Music Theater in Tinley Park, Illinois, and I worked one of the refreshment tents as a close-up magician. Hell, even the aforementioned Buddy Guy and Koko Taylor made the resume. I have no qualms to this day about using these credits. You do what you have to do in order to get noticed in entertainment, and in some cases these little white lies helped get me further along in my career. They helped make it possible for me to actually work on stage with people like Gladys Knight, Louie Anderson, Joey Fatone, Jerry Springer, and many others. Actors don't always mention when they were an extra in a major motion picture. Singers don't always specify if they were on tour or a contracted background singer for a night. Comedians and variety acts don't always mention when they truly worked with a celebrity. That's how it goes.

One of my favorite credits did and didn't actually happen. I, along with countless other comedians, have NBC's popular *Last Comic Standing* listed on my resume. Some have a more legitimate entitlement to the credit than I do. Others have even less reason to claim it on there. Shows like this, or any other popular talent competition show, frequently feature interviews with people waiting in line for their audition, tryout footage of people who don't make it, and massive crowd shots showing the world how many people want to be berated by Simon Cowell. I can say with absolute honesty I was on the very first season of *Last Comic Standing*. Thankfully, I am not stretching the truth by claiming it as a credit by being seen in the crowd, nor was I one of the people briefly interviewed while waiting in the frigid cold. I also wasn't a contestant.

If you watched the show, either on NBC or rebroadcast on Comedy Central, you saw me eating fire on stage in the first and last episodes of season one. I saw it with my own eyes, as did millions of people. I am certain I wasn't on the air for more than 30 seconds total, but I received countless phone calls from friends who saw the show and recognized me. The first episode showed me full-on fire eating in a montage of memorable auditions. On the last episode, I had an actual line and a rather dubious distinction. At the end of the season, they reflected on how far the finalists had come by displaying another montage of auditions from the beginning of the contest. Host Jay Mohr introduced the segment by announcing to the world, "Here's a look at the best . . . of the worst." The clip featured me making a dramatic pass of a lit torch into my mouth, and breathing out a burst of flame as if in mortal pain. With a look of disgust right into the camera, I said, "This job *sucks!*" That always gets a great response from any audience I perform for, and it got a good laugh from the audience at the show's finale. My phone started ringing, and *Last Comic Standing* went on the list. The best part was I didn't have to suffer the indignity of performing stupid stunts, living in a cramped apartment with a bunch of other comics, sharing a bathroom with Ralphie May, or enduring a single moment of Dat Phan making fun of his Asian mother's broken "Engrish." I had a couple new legitimate credits on my resume, since I could say "As seen on NBC *and* Comedy Central" with very little inconvenience or effort. I may not have gotten more famous or well paid, but it did open more doors for me over the years.

The last of the biggies I will share is one I shall always be grateful for, even though I wish it were entirely true. I have been hanging my hat on the fact that I performed for President George H.W. Bush for many years. Any sort of performance for a president is worthy of being on your list of accomplishments. The fact is, George Herbert Walker Bush was not actually in attendance at the Washington Press Club's Salute to the 101st Congress. We had been told he'd be there, we went through the security and protocol training, but shortly before the event began we were told that he couldn't attend due to an illness. However, since his name appeared on several of the programs and press releases for the event, and it certainly was an event where you would expect to see him, he helped sell a very young Andy Martello to prospective clients. I am confident I'm not the only one from that show to have that fake feather in my cap.

While I was upset that I didn't get to juggle or even catch a glimpse of a president, I later altered my resume and stage introductions in a way that turned the credit into a joke. It took quite a few years before I could use the joke, but I still use it to this day.

After George W. Bush took office, I changed the credit to read, "He has even performed for President Bush (The original. NOT the sequel!)". The joke became a clever way of taking a resume lie and making it a credible non-credit. While not the greatest of jokes, it always gets a good laugh and currently stands as the closing line to my stage introduction. Had I never lied about working for a president, I'd have never had an honestly good credit in my introduction. Even a lie can bring about a useful truth.

There you have it. My resume lies have been brought to the foreground; if only to add a little humor and humility to this book. Above all else, you know by now that I am certainly not lying when I tell you: I am absolutely not now, nor have I ever been, famous.

ABOUT THE AUTHOR

Andy Martello is a professional entertainer, comedian, and author living in Las Vegas, Nevada. You have seen him on *American Restoration, Mystery Diners,* and quite briefly on *Last Comic Standing.* In 2016, he was named Best Local Author by *The Las Vegas Review-Journal.* Presently, he tours North America as the announcer for *The Price is Right LIVE!*

His first book, *The King of Casinos: Willie Martello and the El Rey Club,* has won 14 awards and is in development to become a major motion picture.

When reviewing this book on Amazon, look for his other books, *Pretty Words. Nothing More.* and *Andy Martello's Here's Your Host!: Insights and Interviews with Game Show Greats.* Future works include, *Pretty Words. So Much More.,* and *Andy Martello's Roommate Chronicles.*

Website: andymartello.com   Email: andy@andymartello.com
Facebook: facebook.com/andymartelloentertainment
Twitter: Twitter.com/THEandymartello
Goodreads: Goodreads.com/AndyMartello
LIKE and FOLLOW Andy everywhere. Help make him famous.

Made in the USA
Columbia, SC
19 February 2020

88108030R00109